THE ATLANTIC CRITICAL STUDIES

WILLIAM SHAKESPEARE'S

King Lear

THE ATLANTIC CRITICAL STUDIES

WILLIAM SHAKESPEARE'S
King Lear

RATRI RAY

ATLANTIC
PUBLISHERS & DISTRIBUTORS (P) LTD

Published by

ATLANTIC
PUBLISHERS & DISTRIBUTORS (P) LTD

B-2, Vishal Enclave, Opp. Rajouri Garden,
New Delhi-110027
Phones : 25413460, 25429987, 25466842

Sales Office
7/22, Ansari Road, Darya Ganj,
New Delhi-110002
Phones : 23273880, 23275880, 23280451
Fax : 91-11-23285873
web : www.atlanticbooks.com
e-mail : info@atlanticbooks.com

Printed in India
at Nice Printing Press, Delhi

General Preface

The Atlantic Critical Studies, modelled on the study-aids available in England and America, among other places, are primarily meant for the students of English Literature of Indian universities.

However, in consideration of the local conditions and the various constraints under which our students have to study— non-availability of relevant critical books, dearth of foreign and Indian journals, inaccessibility to good, well-equipped libraries, just to mention a few of them—the models have been considerably improved upon, both qualitatively and quantitatively.

Thus, while these studies are meant to be comprehensive and self-sufficient, the distinguished scholars who have prepared these study materials, have taken special care to combine lucidity and profundity in their treatment of the texts.

The Select Bibliography at the end is meant not only to acknowledge the sources used but also to help a student in the pursuit of further studies if s/he wants to.

Atlantic Publishers & Distributors (P) Ltd. believe in quality and excellence. These studies will only reconfirm it.

Mohit K. Ray
Chief Editor [English Literature]
Atlantic Publishers & Distributors,
New Delhi

Contents

Contents

1

Introduction

Shakespeare is indeed such a titanic figure that he defies all kinds of categorisations. If one takes the most superficial and conventional idea of a great poet then Shakespeare does not fit comfortably within it. For example, we usually think that a great poet goes unappreciated by his contemporaries, dies unrecognised and in poverty, and it is the privilege of later generations to discover and acclaim his talents. This does not fit our poet at all, for he was not only recognised as a genius by his contemporaries, but Ben Jonson, one of the greatest figures of his time had declared that he loved Shakespeare "this side idolatry". He did not have a pitiable end in poverty and squalor, but died as one of the richest men of his village. Again, one is in the habit of thinking that great poets are a little weak in their understanding of day-to-day practicalities. Shakespeare was so practical and pragmatic in his attitude to such matters that he came to partially own the theatrical company that staged all his plays, bought the most valuable property in his village and raised his family to the status of landed gentry.

Yet these are but superficialities. As a Bard, a poet, a dramatist, a sonneteer, Shakespeare had no equal in his own time or since then. Within the few years that span his productivity he poured out a wealth of narrative poems, plays and sonnets such as have hardly been met with since. There were many rules and conventions of dramaturgy that had to be followed. Sometimes he did follow them and used them to enhance the effect of his plays. At other times, with the sovereign confidence of a master, he disregarded them and yet produced works that stood the test of time most ably. Different elements of plays, like the plot, the theme, the characters etc. blend in such a way as to harmonise into a many-coloured prismatic radiance. The more assiduously one studies his plays, the more one discovers the undefinability of the nature of critical terms of appreciation like "sublimity", "universality", "esemplastic imagination" etc. which describe only a few of the different aspects of his genius. He remains essentially inexhaustible.

Setting aside his other works, in the field of drama itself there is surprising range and variety. He turned into gold whatever he took up. It cannot be said of any other writer of his time that like Shakespeare he wrote plays of all kinds, tragedies, comedies and histories. Marlowe was his greatest rival and he wrote only tragedies. Ben Jonson, another great figure, could have been a formidable rival, but since he wrote only satirical comedies, he was more of a foil than otherwise. Within the three main genres of contemporary plays, again, Shakespeare shows more variety than any other writer. All the four main categories of tragedy can be found in his works. The Conqueror tragedy is presented in *Macbeth*, the Revenge tragedy in *Hamlet*, the Villain tragedy in *Othello* and the Domestic tragedy in *Romeo and Juliet*. Our present concern *King Lear* is a play that goes beyond all categories. It must always be remembered that these labels are more a matter of convenience than conviction and the genres often overlap.

His tragedies, like his comedies, have been put into different categories, quite apart from the four mentioned above. Keeping in mind the fact that these are made only for the convenience of the historian and the student, they are:

The Early Tragedies: *Titus Andronius, Romeo and Juliet.*
The Great Tragedies: *Hamlet, Othello, King Lear, Macbeth.*
The Roman Tragedies: *Julius Caesar, Antony and Cleopatra, Coriolanus.*

Tragedies, more than any other kinds of play, show the triumph of good over evil. A tragic writer like Shakespeare shows the existence of evil in man and society, and also its ultimate but inevitable defeat. As the French critic Henri Fluchère has pointed out:

> What has always appealed to him with constant tenacity is the sense of order and equilibrium which can be attained only by crushing the forces of evil by the triumph of good.[1]

REFERENCE

1. Fluchère, H., *Shakespeare*, London: Longmans, Green and Co., 1953, p. 264.

2

The Background

(a) The Socio-political Background

No writer stands independent of his time and milieu. The social structure, the political atmosphere, the religious and cultural tradition—everything influences him and his work. Shakespeare, too, was no exception. The authoritative social historian G.M. Trevelyan asserts:

> His works could never have been produced in any other period than those late Elizabethan and early Jacobean periods in which it was his luck to live. He could not have written as he did if the men and women among whom his days were passed had been other than they were.[1]

The socio-political background of any author, thus, bears an integral relationship to his work. We should therefore have a working knowledge of Shakespeare's background. A brief chronological time-table of the main events from Queen Elizabeth's succession to the death of our poet is given below. It contains, in brief, the chief political, social and religious events of the time. The last of these three is important because religion was an important issue of the time and influenced people's lives. Some events on the continent have also been mentioned.

A CHRONOLOGICAL TABLE

1558 – Queen Mary I dies. Elizabeth I succeeds.

      – Mary Queen of the Scots marries the French Dauphin.

'59 – Mary Queen of the Scots declares herself the Queen of England, in spite of Queen Elizabeth.

- War between Spain and France ends.
- The Church of England re-established more firmly.

'60 - The Scottish Parliament establishes the Reformed church and breaks with Rome and the Pope.

'61 - Mary Queen of Scots returns from France.
- She clashes with the Calvinists.

'62 - The Huguenots start emigrating from France to England.

'63 - Bubonic plague in Europe.

'64 - *Shakespeare born.* Galileo born.
- England is at war with Spain.
- The Thirty-Nine Articles adopted by the Church of England. Queen Elizabeth makes a laudable attempt to enforce uniformity of religion.

'67 - Mary Queen of the Scots abdicates.
- Rugby Chapel founded.

'68 - Mary Queen of the Scots flees to England and is held captive by Queen Elizabeth.

'69 - Rebellion of the Roman Catholic earls crushed.

'70 - Pope Pius V excommunicates Queen Elizabeth.

'74 - Burbage gets licence for the first theatre in London.

'76 - Tycho Brahe begins his astronomical observations.
- Burbage opens the first theatre in London.

'77 - Treaty with the Dutch signed.
- Sir Francis Drake begins his circumnavigation of the world.

'80 - Sir Francis Drake completes circumnavigation.

'81 - Conversion to Catholicism declared to be treason.
- Galileo discovers the Law of the Pendulum.

'83 - Plot against the Queen's life discovered and scotched.
- Humphrey Gilbert takes possession of Newfoundland in the name of the Queen.

'84 – Sir Walter Raleigh discovers Virginia and names it after the Queen. He arranges for colonisation.

'86 – England wins the battle of Zutphen. Sir Philip Sidney dies in this battle.

– Plot against the Queen in which Mary Queen of the Scots is implicated, and convicted of treason.

'87 – Rose Theatre built by Henslowe.

'88 – Defeat of the Spanish Armada by Sir Francis Drake.

'89 – Galileo publishes the result of his experiments with falling bodies.

'92 – John Davis discovers the Falkland islands.

'93 – Absence from the Church on Sundays made punishable by law.

'95 – Robert Southwell the mystical poet executed for celebrating Mass.

'96 – England, France and Netherlands form alliance against Spain.

'97 – Irish Rebellion. Statutory provision for Poor Relief. Beggary made illegal.

'98 – The Bodleian Library begun. The Globe Theatre opened.

1603 – Queen Elizabeth dies. Accession of King James I.

'04 – Peace with Spain. Acts against priests and recusants. Anglican canons made.

'05 – Repression of Puritans and Catholics. Gunpowder plot.

'08 – Failure for the King in his plans for union with Scotland.

'10 – Judicial decision against royal proclamations.

'11 – The Parliament is dissolved.

'12 – Alliance with German Protestant princes.

– Witches hanged at Lancashire.

1616 – *Shakespeare dies.*

Though this table is very sketchy, yet a careful study of it will reveal the main features of the contemporary socio-political situation. When Shakespeare was born the throne of England was in a very unstable condition. There were plots against the Queen by her own subjects while abroad there was constant warfare with the neighbouring nations. Quite a few years passed before the Queen could feel comparative security on the throne and turn her attention to bringing political stability to England in her relationships with her immediate neighbours. The policies that the Queen adopted, both at home and abroad, were wise and tolerant and she brought peace and stability to her country. Under her benevolent governance, even the vexatious and bloody controversies over religion came to an end. Perhaps the most signal achievement of her reign was the establishing of a definite and uniform religious discipline in England. G.M. Trevelyan points out:

> In the year in which the Queen succeeded her sister Mary, Puritanism was mainly a foreign doctrine imported from Geneva and Rhineland; when she died it was rootedly and characteristically English.[2]

Today the Elizabethan Age is known as an age of peace, prosperity and expansion in every field. As far as the social framework is concerned class barriers did exist, but it was an accepted feature, not resented by anyone. This was because the feudal lords rarely oppressed any of those who were in their power. It was a healthy society as described by G.M. Trevelyan:

> English society was based not on equality but freedom— freedom of opportunity and freedom of personal intercourse. Such was the Engand known and approved by Shakespeare.[3]

Each member of this society had self-reliance and self-respect, for he earned a fair wage for honest labour. No bondmen or slaves existed.

Industry and trade also prospered. The factory system had come into existence. The capitalist employer provided jobs to a great number of men as he was anxious to keep his factory working at full capacity. Mining expanded to a very great extent so that metals like lead, copper, iron and tin became available to all.

National pride climbed a high peak as a result of the two remarkable achievements of Sir Francis Drake – the defeat of the hitherto invincible Spanish Armada and the circumnavigation of the world. The sense of joy and exuberance which pervaded England is reflected in the literature of the time:

> By the end of Elizabeth's reign not only was England commercially and financially reviving and expanding on a modern basis but her ancient rivals were in rapid decline.[4]

(b) The Literary Background

Not for nothing is the Elizabethan Age known as the Golden Age of England. As such Elizabethan England invites comparison with Periclean Greece and Augustan Rome. As has been explained in the foregoing section the age was a prosperous one from the social point of view and it was even more so as far as literature was concerned. A chronological table is given below which covers the main literary events of the time. It begins with the first performance of *Ralph Roister Doister* which took place ten years before Shakespeare's birth. His own plays are not mentioned here as they will be given later. (*Vide* Chapter 3, *Life and Works, infra*)

A CHRONOLOGICAL TABLE

1554 – Sir Philip Sidney and Lyly born.
       – *Ralph Roister Doister* performed.
'57 – Tottel's *Miscellany*. Lord North's *The Dial of Princes*.
'58 – Kyd, Greene, Peele, Lodge born.
'61 – Bacon born. *Gorboduc* performed.
'63 – Drayton and Donne born.
'64 – Shakespeare born. Marlowe born.
'66 – *Supposes* by Gascoigne. Painter's *Palace of Pleasure*.
'67 – Campion and Nashe born. Pickering's *Interlude of Vice*.
'75 – Heywood and Tourneur born. *Appius and Virginia*, *Gammer Gurton's Needle*.
'76 – *Paradyse of Daynty Devises*.

'77 – Holinshed's *Chronicles*. Grange's *Golden Aphroditis*.
'78 – Lyly's *Euphues*.
'79 – Spenser's *Shepheardes Calender*. Gosson's *Schole of Abuse*.
'82 – Hakluyt's *Voyages*.
'85 – Kyd's *The Spanish Tragedy*.
'86 – Sir Philip Sidney dies. Lyly's *Endimion*.
'87 – Marlowe's *Tamburlaine*, Lyly's *Gallathea*.
'89 – Marlowe's *Jew of Malta*. Puttenham's *Arte of English Poesie*.
'90 – *Faerie Queene* Bks I-III, Sidney's *Arcadia*.
'91 – *Astrophel and Stella*, Marlowe's *Edward II*.
'92 – Daniel's *To Delia*, Marlowe's *Hero and Leander*.
'95 – Spenser's *Amorletti* and *Epithalamion*. Sidney's *Apology for Poetry*.
'99 – Spenser dies. Ben Jonson's *Every Man Out of His Humour*.
'1600 – *England's Helicon*. Ben Jonson's *Cynthia's Revels*.
'01 – Dekker and Marston's *Satiromastix*. Jonson's *Poetaster*.
'03 – Dowland's *Third Book of Songs*, *Sejanus*.
'04 – Chapman's *Bussy D'Ambois*, Marston's *Malcontent*.
'05 – Drayton's *Collected Poems*.
'06 – Lyly dies. *Yorkshire Tragedy*, *Volpone*, *Revenger's Tragedy*.
'07 – Beaumont and Fletcher's *Knight of the Burning Pestle*.
'09 – *Philaster*, Fulke Greville's *Mustapha*.
'10 – Ben Jonson's *The Alchemist*.
'11 – *The Authorised Version of The Bible*.
'12 – Chapman's *Iliad*, Webster's *The White Devil*.
'13 – Overbury and Constable die. *Purchas His Pilgrimage*.
'14 – Overbury's *Characters*, Lodge's *Works of Seneca*,

Raleigh's *History of the World*, Jonson's
Bartholomew Fair, Webster's *Duchess of Malfi*.

'16 – *Shakespeare dies*. Chapman's *The Whole Works of
Homer*, Jonson's *Works*, his *Devil is an Ass*.

(This table mentions only a few of the works written and
published during this time.)

As can be seen from this table, the years covering
Shakespeare's birth in 1564 to his death in 1616 were the most
productive ones. During Sidney's lifetime the most notable
works had not yet come into existence and so his *Apologie for
Poetry* decries English drama. The state of English literature,
however, improved by leaps and bounds, the drama most of all.
During our poet's childhood many plays were already being
written and staged, all of an inferior kind. Only *Gorboduc* is
praised by Sidney:

> ...as it is full of stately speeches and well-sounding phrases,
> climbing to the heights of Seneca's style and as full of
> notable morality which it doth most delightfully teach, and
> so obtain the very end of poesy.[5]

In 1587 a play was performed by a group of eight authors
(among whom was included Lord Bacon), for the Queen's
entertainment. Entitled *The Misfortunes of King Arthur*, today
this play has only historical value. This was the childhood of
Elizabethan drama, to be soon outsourced by Marlowe,
Shakespeare and all the others.

Shakespeare had pre-existing models to follow, and
occasionally improve upon, not only in drama but in sonnets,
songs and narrative poems as well. In this respect also the early
Elizabethan Age presents a prospect marginally better than the
prospect of drama. Spenser's *Shepheardes Calender* and the first
few books of *Faerie Queene* had been published before our poet
wrote his *Venus and Adonis*, his first narrative poem. The
Sonnets of Wyatt and Surrey had been published by Tottel in his
Miscellany. It was only in the last decade of the century that the
famous sonnet-sequences were written. From 1680 onwards the
countless love-songs started to be written, and were published
under attractive names: *Paradyse of Daynty Devises*, *England's*

Helicon are but two of them. The poets are mostly anonymous and go under the name of "the Elizabethan nest of singing-birds." After giving a list of the features of these lyrics Yvor Winters says:

> The best poems in the early school are among the most perfect examples of the classical virtues to be found in English poetry.[6]

The Elizabethan Age, as it progressed, brought forth a scintillating wealth of many kinds of poems: narrative, lyrical, discursive, religious etc. Prose, too, flourished in the hands of writers like Lord Bacon, Sir Thomas Browne, Burton, Hooker and others.

In the present instance, drama is of great interest. Here, in tragedy, the prevailing influence was that of Seneca. Kyd's famous *The Spanish Tragedy*, which became the prototype for all revenge tragedies, was in the Senecan mode. Another such popular tragedy was *Tamburlaine* by Marlowe. This was so successful that Marlowe had to produce a sequel and both bear the imprint of his artistic talent. Burbage and later Henslowe established theatre halls where plays came to be regularly performed and became one of the chief sources of entertainment for the Elizabethan public. The great dramatists experimented with different kinds of plays and honed their skills to perfection. Tragedies of four different kinds, comedies catering to three distinct classes, chronicle plays and farces were poured forth in an endless stream. Besides Shakespeare, the late Elizabethan Age produced the works of many others, though drama reached its highest peak towards the end of the Elizabethan age, and the beginning of the Jacobean. Ben Jonson, Webster, Chapman, Tourneur, Middleton, Marston, Dekker, Heywood—these are the names of some of the most popular dramatists.

The tragedies of this time have been designated as the Blood-and-thunder tragedies and divided into four categories. Conqueror tragedies centred around an overwhelmingly ambitious person, like the tragedies of Marlowe. The Revenge tragedy was started by Kyd and started proliferating immediately after. Villain tragedy was the third kind, *The Changeling* of

Middleton and Rowley being a very fine example. Our poet's *Othello* is often categorised as one. The fourth kind of tragedy was the domestic tragedy. The two anonymous plays, *The Yorkshire Tragedy* and *Arden of Feversham* are examples of this last kind.

Comedy is not very important in the present instance but it may be noted that different kinds of comedies flourished during the period. Shakespeare himself had written three kinds of comedies: the romantic, the problem comedies and the romances. He did not try his hand at the satirical city comedies in which Ben Jonson excelled. Tragi-comedies were being written by Beaumont and Fletcher. There was thus, great variety in tragedy as well as in comedy.

Another kind of play being written at this time was the chronicle play or the history play. This is a kind of play that cannot be labelled as a tragedy or a comedy but exists in its own right. Some of them, like Marlowe's *Edward II* ends in the death of the hero, causing it to be called a historical tragedy. This is the case with some of Shakespeare's own history plays as well, specially *Richard II*. Not many writers wrote successful chronicle plays. Shakespeare, with his splendid pageant of historical heroes, remained unrivalled in this field, no one equalled him.

Another form of popular entertainment was the masque. These were very popular and were specially suited for celebrating happy occasions like betrothals, marriages etc. Mythical and supernatural characters like gods and goddesses, nymphs and satyrs were brought on the stage and this naturally involved the use of sumptuous costumes. Such productions were very expensive and were usually produced by the court and the aristocracy. In Queen Elizabeth's court, the noble lords and ladies themselves participated. Ben Jonson wrote many well-known masques. They are to be found incorporated within the framework of Shakespeare's plays also. The masque celebrating the betrothal of Ferdinand and Miranda in *The Tempest* is a well-known example of Shakespeare's use of the masque to enhance the beauty of his plays.

Apart from these there were the farces, causing boisterous

laughter. It was usually from the lower section of society that the characters for farces were taken. Shakespeare did not favour this form. It was only once that he wrote such a play. Queen Elizabeth had been charmed by Sir John Falstaff of Shakespeare's history play *King Henry IV*, Pt I and had specially commissioned a play showing "the fat knight in love." *The Merry Wives of Windsor* was the play our poet wrote to please his sovereign and it is usually taken to be a farce – the only such of Shakespeare.

The times in which Shakespeare wrote, thus, were times that showed the expansion and efflorescence of England in every respect. The form of drama reached a height of excellence rarely touched since then. As F.P. Wilson explains:

> The drama is at its greatest during those years between 1590 and 1620 when the actors were neither poverty-stricken vagabonds nor hangers-on at Court, and when the audience was most representative of City, Country and Court.[7]

REFERENCES

1. Trevelyan, G.M., *Illustrated English Social History*, Vol. 2. Harmondsworth: Penguin Books Ltd., p. 125.

2. *Ibid.*, p. 86.

3. *Ibid.*, p. 62.

4. *Ibid.*, p. 123.

5. Sir Philip Sidney, *An Apology for Poetry*, in Enright, D.J. and Chickera, Ernst de, eds., *English Critical Texts*. Oxford: O.U.P., Twenty-first Impr., 2002, p. 40.

6. Winters, Y., *The Sixteenth Century Lyric in England*, in Alpers, P.J., ed., *Elizabethan Poetry*. Oxford: O.U.P., 1967, p. 96.

7. Wilson, F.P., *Elizabethan and Jacobean Drama*, in Kaufmann, R.J., ed., *Elizabethan Drama*. Oxford: O.U.P., 1961, pp. 4-5.

3

Life and Works

(a) A Short Biography

Many of the great Elizabethan writers remain enigmatic figures since very little is known of their personal life. This is not quite the case with Shakespeare. There is a wealth of biographical material in his case, and one can be certain of many important dates and events. Irving Ribner, pointing out this feature, has also explained it:

> As a dramatist Shakespeare acquired considerable reputation during his own lifetime. It continued to grow in the centuries following his death in 1616, accumulating as it did an accretion of legends and anecdotes.[1]

First of all, a chronological table of the important events of Shakespeare's life is given below.

A CHRONOLOGICAL TABLE OF SHAKESPEARE'S LIFE

1564 – Apr. 23, the supposed date of birth of Shakespeare.

       – Apr. 26, Shakespeare is baptised at the parish church.

'71 – Possible time of enrolment in the local Grammar School.

'78 – His father suffers severe financial loss.

'82 – Shakespeare is married to Anne Hathaway.

'83 – Birth of Susannah, his first daughter.

'85 – Baptism of the twins, Hamnet and Judith.

'86 – His supposed departure for London.

'93 – *Venus and Adonis* published by a fellow villager.

'94   – *Rape of Lucrece, Titus Andronicus.*

'96   – Tragic death of Hamnet his only son, at 12 years.

'97   – He buys New Place, the second largest property.

'99   – He buys shares in the Globe Theatre.

1602 – The birth of his first grandchild. He also buys one hundred and seven acres of land.

'04   – His company comes under royal patronage and is given the name of the King's Men.

'11   – He retires from the company and comes back to settle in his native village.

'13   – *The Tempest* staged.

'16   – Jan. 25 – His Last Will and Testament drawn up.

      – Apr. 23 – He dies on his fifty-second birthday.

      – Apr. 25 – Buried in the Chancel of Stratford Church.

The exact date of his birth is not known, but the date of his christening had been recorded in the Register of Baptism in the parish church of Stratford-upon-Avon, in official Latin:

1564, Apr. 26, Gulielmus Filius Johannes Shakespeare.[2]

Usually a baby was christened three days after its birth, and so it is generally assumed that our poet was born on the twenty-third of April at Stratford-upon-Avon, in the county of Warwickshire. This was, according to the saints' calendar, the auspicious St. George's Day, who is the patron saint of England.

Though nothing is known about his infancy, it can be safely assumed that he had a normal, secure and happy childhood. He was the eldest son and as such he had a strong position in the family. His father, John Shakespeare, was a prosperous tradesman and his mother, Mary Arden, came from a family socially slightly higher than that of his father's. John Shakespeare was not only a prosperous trader, he was also a man of high integrity and this was valued by the village. He gradually rose higher and higher in the social scale and finally became the mayor of Stratford and the alderman in 1565. This was such a high position that he could claim the status of a gentleman. This meant the landed gentry as differentiated from a trader. Shakespeare's came from such a family. This is of great importance in a feudal society.

The village in which he spent his infancy and youth was surrounded by unspoilt countryside. He retained vivid memories of this and reproduced it repeatedly in his works in wonderful verbal pictures. The foundation of the descriptions of nature were laid at this time in the mind of the child.

His father was a Justice of Peace and also the High Bailiff of his village. As such he had to take active part in judicial matters. It is thought by the biographers that Shakespeare, as soon as he was old enough, accompanied him to the law courts and thus gained first-hand knowledge of legal procedures.

The establishment of Grammar Schools, which had been started by the Queen in the second half of the century had by this time become part and parcel of life. Stratford also had its own Grammar School in which the classics were taught. It can hardly be said with assurance exactly when our poet entered this school. According to some he was but seven and according to others nine. He was, however, enrolled in this school where he acquired his store of knowledge. Ben Jonson's opinion that he had only "small Latin and less Greek" is well-known, but actually Shakespeare's knowledge of the classics was not contemptible by any means. He studied in this school for at least seven years. As to at what age he left the school, the biographers do not agree. Whatever he studied there was retained in his memory and repeatedly used in all his works, whether in the large scope of a history play, or in a small reference to classical myths.

There are reliable records of the workings of the schools of this age. Classes started at six in the morning in summer and at seven in winter, and continued till five in the evening. There were, however, frequent breaks during the day, which came up to a total of two and a half hours. The curriculum consisted mainly of Latin grammar and literature. The following works were prescribed:

Poetry: Mantuan's imitation of Virgil named the *Bucolica*,

>Virgil's own *Eclogues* and *The Aeneid*. Horace's
>*Poems* and Ovid's *Metamorphoses*.
>
>*Prose*:   Caesar, Livy and Cicero.
>
>*Drama*: Seneca's tragedies, and the comedies of Plautus
>and Terence.

All these works were studied in their original Latin. A knowledge
of the language therefore, was taken for granted. Irving Ribner
comments on the surprising amount of classical literature
imparted to the schoolboys:

>In the light of the training a normal schoolboy would have
>undergone at the Stratford Grammar School, it is difficult
>to understand why the extent of Shakespeare's learning has
>been so much a subject for debate.[3]

There is, however, another opinion, totally different, about
Shakespeare's schooling. John Dover Wilson holds that
Shakespeare did not attend any of these schools, for they were
all run by Protestants, whereas his family was a staunch
Catholic. Dover Wilson is of the opinion that John Shakespeare
would have put his son in the service of a Catholic nobleman.
He would have, in such a case, got his education along with
the sons of the house and also gained first-hand knowledge of
the lifestyle of the aristocracy.

Knowledge from the schoolbooks was not the only
knowledge that Shakespeare got at this time. He soaked up
knowledge from other sources as well. One such source was
the watching of the plays put up by travelling actors. The great
noblemen of the time, specially the Earls of Leicester and of
Warwickshire (Shakespeare's own county) patronised theatrical
groups which put up plays all over the country. Many such
groups visited his village and he must have seen many plays.

It is definitely known that he came across Anne Hathaway
in his eighteenth year. She herself was fully twenty-six at the
time, but she charmed him and they got married on Nov. 28,
1582. Their first daughter Susannah, was born next year, and
the twins, Hamnet and Judith, two years later. Nothing is
known of Shakespeare's married life. Hamnet died in 1596 at
twelve years of age. No one was left to carry on the line.

By the time that Shakespeare was twenty-one, he was already a married man with a wife and no less than three children to support. It was necessary to find some means of livelihood and there are many stories of his activities at this time. It is said that he was holding a teacher's job at a school near his village, and it is also said that he was acting in a theatrical company. There is one anecdote which is generally accepted, though it may not be true. This story says that Shakespeare and a few other young men had poached in the preserves of Sir Thomas Lucy. Shakespeare was caught and put into prison. Perhaps he was whipped or threatened with whipping. It may be that this incident made him decide to leave the village and go to London in search of a livelihood.

It was probably in 1586 that he came to London. It is not known for sure how he spent his life for the next six years. These are known as the Dark years and there are many theories about them. Perhaps he held the horses of the noblemen who came to the theatre, perhaps he had managed to get a job of some kind in the theatre. It is known however, that he came into contact with one Richard Field, a young man from his own village. Field had become an established printer in London. It was he who published *Venus and Adonis* in 1593 and *The Rape of Lucrece* next year.

The chronological table of the literary background (Chapter 2, *supra*) shows that Shakespeare and Marlowe were born in the same year. They also reached London at very much the same time. The 1580s was a glorious decade for Elizabethan England. Pioneering work was being done in the field of the arts as well as in geography. *Astrophel and Stella*, the first sequence of love-sonnets, was being composed by Sir Philip Sidney and Spenser, in Ireland, was writing *The Faerie Queene*. London was the cultural centre of the country and young men of talent from all over England were converging there. Lyly, having achieved fame with his *Euphues*, had turned his attention to drama. Two of his comedies had been presented to the Queen. The University Wits, Thomas Kyd, Robert Greene and Thomas Nashe had all settled in London. Marlowe achieved instant fame by *Tamburlaine* in 1587. It was an exhilarating time, with new horizons opening out in all directions. F.E. Halliday describes the time:

> It was a proud, mercurial, quarrelsome vivid society, a mediaeval people magically vitalised by contact with the Renaissance, quivering with energy.[4]

Shakespeare quickly became part of this heady London life and started the slow climb to fame. It is paradoxical that the first mention of his name in London should be due to professional jealousy. It is given by Greene in a work which is remembered only for this reference—a spiteful one, to Shakespeare.

It is a pamphlet called *Greene's Groatsworth of Wit bought with a Million of Repentances*, and contains, at the end, a letter addressed to his friends Marlowe, Nashe and Peele. Greene cautions them against actors:

> Yes, trust them not: for there is an upstart crow, beautified with our feathers that with his Tyger's heart wrapt in a player's hyde, supposes he is as well able to bombast out a blank verse as the best of you; and being an absolute Johannes fac totum, is in his own conceit the only Shakescene in a country.[5]

This gives two clear references to Shakespeare. First of all there is the name Shake—scene and secondly the line "Tyger's heart wrapt in a Player's hyde" which is an adaptation of a line in Shakespeare's popular trilogy *Henry VI*, Part III: "O tiger's heart, wrapped in a woman's hide." This malicious backbiting serves to make us realise that Shakespeare was becoming well-known in the theatrical world—enough to cause alarm and jealousy in the well-established University Wits.

These early years are today known as his time of apprenticeship and were highly productive. The two myth-based narrative poems *Venus and Adonis* and the *Rape of Lucrece* were written at this time as well as the sonnet-sequence dedicated to Mr W.H. *The Henry VI* trilogy, *Richard III*, *Titus Andronicus*, *The Comedy of Errors*, *The Two Gentlemen of Verona* and *The Taming of the Shrew* were all written at this time. The plays were highly successful on the stage. *Titus Andronicus*, one of his least attractive plays was so popular that it came to be performed by the three best companies of the time, those patronised by the Earls of Derby, Pembroke and Sussex. As has been pointed out earlier (*Vide* Chapter 1, *Introduction*, *supra*), many playwrights were writing at this time, but all of them had a limited range. Kyd and Marlowe wrote highly popular tragedies and there their talents drew rein. Shakespeare was the only one who could give, even at this early stage, histories, tragedies and comedies with equal facility. By 1594 he had hardly anyone to equal him, whether in drama, poems or sonnets.

There were many theatrical groups in London at this time and the best of them was the one known as the Lord Chamberlaine's Men. Shakespeare became the writer of this group and thus held a position of great importance. Every group depended on its writer for its success and survival, just as the writer needed the group. Shakespeare continued in this healthy symbiotic relationship with this group till his retirement.

Even before he was thirty he had become a highly successful man. He came to Stratford and stayed there for four months. By this time his children were of an age to need schooling, and his father was an old man of sixty. It is thought that both *Venus and Adonis* and *Richard III* were written here.

It was at this time that one of the most important relationships of his life took root. He met Henry Wriothesley, the Earl of Southampton. This handsome aristocrat was nearly ten years younger than him, and an enthusiastic patron of arts. An intense relationship developed between Shakespeare and him, expressed in his sonnets. Both of the narrative poems are dedicated to him and Shakespeare professes, in the Dedication, a deep and enduring love for his patron. Different aspects of this relationship are expressed in the sonnets. The Earl's patronage gave Shakespeare, not only one of the most intense experiences of his life, but security. A.L. Rowse, pointing out the difference between him and the other poets in respect of social security, says:

It meant all the difference between the dreadful insecurity

poor Greene and others had died of, and having firm ground under his feet.[6]

This means that Shakespeare was financially secure then, with a prosperous artistic career to look forward to. He bought a share in his company which, besides making money for the public performances, also performed at Court, and this brought honour. London was being annually ravaged by the Plague and Shakespeare was the only dramatist to survive it. Kyd was already dead. Peele would die in a few years. Lyly and Lodge had discontinued writing for the stage and Nashe had drifted away to writing pamphlets. Marlowe would have been a worthy rival, but he was killed in a drunken brawl in a tavern. The only playwright with genius nearly equal to his own was Ben Jonson, but he had not started to write yet. Shakespeare, thus, was without a rival either on the stage or in life. It is true that in the sonnets he mentions a rival, but perhaps it was Marlowe, who died soon after.

His comedies offered exactly the kind of light-hearted entertainment that the audience wanted. The exuberant and musical comedies *Love's Labour Lost*, *A Midsummer Night's Dream* and *The Merchant of Venice* enthralled the audience. The university students had taken Shakespeare to their bosom. There are rapturous references to him in a poem by Henry Willoughby, an Oxford undergraduate who was clearly an admirer:

Yet Tarquin plucked his glistering grape
And Shakespeare paints poor Lucrece's rape.[7]

Fame and success was his, but tragedy was lurking very near. In 1597 he was at Stratford when his only son Hamnet died. The family line ended here.

Shakespeare was so prosperous by this time that he was able to buy New Place, which was the second best property in Stratford. He could now claim the status of landed gentry. His father had applied to the Herald's College some years ago for a coat-of-arms. Shakespeare followed it up and the request was granted. So he came back to London as a member of the landed gentry.

There is a famous reference to him and his works in *Palladis Tamia* by Francis Meres, written in 1598. Meres compares him with classical Roman dramatists Plautus and Seneca in the fields of comedy and tragedy respectively:

> As Plautus and Seneca are accounted the best for Comedy and Tragedy among the Latines: Shakespeare among the English is the most excellent for both kinds.[8]

This work is of great value as it mentions the two narrative poems, "the sugred sonnets", and eleven of his play, thus dating them firmly.

King James's accession to the throne was a great event, for he took Shakespeare's company under his wing. It became known as the King's Men, the highest honour in the land. Hereafter can be found many records of this time of his life, presenting the picture of a busy, popular and creative person.

The four great tragedies were written at this time. *Hamlet* was the last of the plays produced in the time of Elizabeth and *Othello* was performed in 1604 in King James's court. While 1606 saw the staging of *King Lear* and *Macbeth*. Along with the tragedies the Problem comedies and the Chronicle plays were also being written and performed. There is a notable change of tone in his works of this time. A sombre note has crept in, ousting exuberance:

> The Jacobean poetry.... is one of compression and lacks the definition of the Elizabethan; thought is packed tight and imagery reduced to the single word of metaphors.[9]

His first grandchild was born in 1608 and it was in this year that his mother passed away. Next year, in 1609, his sonnets which had been in circulation for about a decade in manuscript form, were now published. He started writing his last Romances. In 1611 he retired from his company and settled in his native village as a prosperous and respected man.

Retirement did not mean inaction, for he continued coming to London. His name occurs in many of the documents of this time. In 1612 there was a royal betrothal and *The Tempest* was staged on this occasion. It is thought that Shakespeare himself enacted the role of Prospero.

His time was running out now and in Jan. 1616 his will was drawn up. A few months later, on his birthday, the twenty-third of April, he breathed his last. This was his fifty-second birth anniversary. There is an elaborate tomb on his grave, with his coat-of-arms and many allegorical figures and inscriptions. The most well-known of these is an epitaph in the shape of a quatrain, thought to have been written by him:

Good friend, for Jesus sake forbeare,

To dig the dust enclosed here!

Blest be the man yt spares the stones,

And curst be he yt moves my bones.[10]

(b) Shakespeare's Works

It has not been always possible to get the exact date of each of his works. The dates of performances can be obtained with fair accuracy. Henslowe used to make entries in his *Diary* of the dates of the performances. The Stationer's Register also has entries. Basing the dates on these and other documents, modern scholars have divided his career into four phases as given below. The phases, however, should not be treated like water-tight compartments, for there are possible overlappings.

PHASE I

1591 – *The Comedy of Errors.*

'92 – *The Two Gentlemen of Verona, Henry VI, Pts I, II, III.*

'93 – *Richard III, Romeo and Juliet, Venus and Adonis.*

PHASE II

'94 – *The Rape of Lucrece, The Sonnets, Titus Andronicus, King Richard II, A Midsummer Night's Dream, Love's Labour's Lost, The Taming of the Shrew, King John.*

'95 – *The Merchant of Venice.*

'97 – *Henry IV, Part I.*

'98 – *Henry IV, Part II, The Merry Wives of Windsor.*

'98 – *King Henry V, Much Ado About Nothing, Julius Caesar.*

1600 – *As You Like It, Twelfth Night.*

PHASE III

1602 – *Hamlet, Troilus and Cressida, All's Well that Ends Well.*
'04 – *Measure for Measure, Othello.*
'05 – *King Lear.*
'06 – *Macbeth.*
'07 – *Antony and Cleopatra.*
'08 – *Coriolanus, Timon of Athens, Pericles.*

PHASE IV

'10 – *Cymbeline, The Winter's Tale, The Tempest.*
'11 – *Henry VIII.*

The different phases, as given above, melt into each other and have been designated according to his artistic development. The first one is that of Experiment and goes on till 1594. According to some critics it can be extended to 1595 when *The Merchant of Venice* was written. During this period our poet was engaged primarily in re-writing old plays. There are many traces of immaturity, specially in the style. Yet it cannot be denied that the poetry of this time is rich and exuberant. There is a considerable amount of ornamentation and play on words. The characters lack in depth.

Next comes the phase of development, which stretches from 1595 to 1601. He is enjoying the security and self-respect that the patronage of the Earl of Southampton has brought to him. The struggle for establishing himself is over and he can turn his attention to the perfecting of his art. He, having fully mastered the technique of dramatic blank verse, can now modulate it to the demands of each individual character. As a result the characters gradually become more realistic, giving evidence of deep psychological insight. The plots of the history plays as well as those of the golden comedies show how adept he has become at collecting material from many different sources and arranging and adapting them to his own advantage.

The prevailing mood of the third phase is a sombre and gloomy one. His attention is now focused on the frailties of human nature and the unavoidable presence of evil. This preoccupation is reflected not only in the tragedies but in the comedies also which, for this reason, are called the Dark Comedies as contrasted with the earlier group which is known as the Golden or the Happy Comedies.

But, being a man and an artist of extraordinary mental powers, Shakespeare triumphed over all this to emerge into the peace and tranquillity of the last phase. Here is the evidence of a fully mature wisdom that accepts the presence of evil along with goodness. The Romances he wrote during this time illustrate this wisdom.

(c) Notes on Individual Works

The Comedy of Errors

This is the shortest of his plays and is at present thought by the scholars to be his first. It is modelled on *Menaechmi*, a well-known comedy of Plautus. Even in this first play Shakespeare's stage sense is in evidence, for he has altered Plautus's plot. In the Plautine play there is but one pair of twins but our poet has introduced two. The play is a hilarious comedy based on mistaken identities, and Shakespeare's play, having two pairs of twins, is naturally far more complicated. It is not known when it was performed first, but it was presented at Court in 1594. Critics agree that it might have been put up on the public stage before this.

The Two Gentlemen of Verona

Some scholars think that this is his first play. Whether that is right or not, this is definitely the first of his romantic comedies. The characters are balanced with each other, for there are two fathers, two servants and two pairs of lovers. This makes for a well-balanced, symmetrical plot. There are two themes here – that of friendship and that of love. The stress falls on the former. Two themes of a highly serious nature, which will occupy him till the very end of his career, those of forgiveness and reconciliation, occur here for the first time. An important Shakespearean character, that of the Clown, occurs here.

Henry VI, Pts I, II and III

Here indeed, Shakespeare has no parallel in the creation of the patriotic and colourful pageants. These are not mere depiction of historical events, for he takes up the serious issues of kingship and its many responsibilities. The material for the history plays came from Holinshed's *Chronicles*. This trilogy was so popular that it was performed, in 1592, three times in eight days. Reaching its climax in regicide, the cycle presents a world of betrayal and conflict. Shakespeare was already becoming a threat to the University. Wits as can be seen in Greene's spiteful reference to one of the lines in this trilogy, "O tiger's heart wrapped in a woman's hide" (*Vide* the section on *Life*).

Richard III

This is more of a tragedy than a history play. The hero, King Richard III, is a Marlovian figure. This shows that Shakespeare is still under the influence of Marlowe, for the earlier *Henry VI* trilogy also had given evidence of Marlowe's influence in its poetry. In this play it is the character that shows the influence. King Richard III however, is a far more complex figure than Marlowe's heroes. This shows that Shakespeare's psychological insight is already deeper than that of Marlowe and that his poetry is strong enough to portray this complexity. This is the second longest play of our poet, *Hamlet* being the longest.

Romeo and Juliet

The first of his romantic tragedies, this play tells the story of conflict between two families in which a pair of star-crossed lovers is caught. Here it is Fate, more than character, that dominates the action. "Character is destiny" is the maxim generally applied to Elizabethan tragedies, but it is not applicable in this case. Shakespeare took up an Italian story and followed it quite closely. The character of Mercutio is an original one, for there is no such character in the story that he followed. The pair of lovers has passed into common life as the very symbol of young lovers. Shakespeare's power of

versification is already making itself felt, specially in the Queen
Mab speech of Mercutio.

Venus and Adonis

Narrative poems based on Greek myths were very popular in
those days. This poem became so highly appreciated that it ran
through ten or eleven editions. It amply proves the versatility of
his genius. It is composed in sextains, i.e., iambic pentametre
quatrain followed by a couplet and Shakespeare shows himself
to be a master of this form. Many such poems were being
written at this time and Shakespeare had models enough to
guide him. Though it was a new field for him, he takes up the
form of "erotic epyllion" and shows himself to be a master at
it. He is as much at home in drama as in the form of a lyrical
and sensuous love-story in a complex stanza-pattern.

The Rape of Lucrece

This was published in the year following that of his first
narrative poem, Venus and Adonis. This, too, like the former,
is based on classical myths, and, like the former, was dedicated
to the Earl of Southampton. The stanza-form is more complex
than that used in the former. It is in rhyme royal, a stanza of
seven iambic pentametre lines in an intricate rhyme-scheme.
The figure of Tarquin is presented with great psychological
insight so that he becomes a tragic character. This complexity
raises the poem far above the level of a merely well-written
and entertaining story. The poet's own personality shines
through the classical panoply.

The Sonnets

The love-sonnet sequence was one of the most popular
poetic forms of the time and Shakespeare uses the prevailing
fashion to write one of his most intensely emotional works. It
is a sequence of a hundred and fifty-four sonnets. The entire
sequence is dedicated to "the onlie begetter" Mr. W.H. who is
not named more specifically. The majority of the sonnets is
addressed to him and the rest to an equally mysterious Dark
Lady. Many were the sequences produced at that time, but
none of them can approach Shakespeare's in intensity of
emotion or in the beauty of expression.

Titus Andronicus

This is a revenge tragedy in the Senecan tradition which was popularised by Kyd. It is a typical blood-and-thunder tragedy supplying exactly what the audience wanted, but too crude for modern tastes. Kyd's *The Spanish Tragedy* guided Shakespeare as far as the technique and the theme of revenge are concerned, but it is clear that our poet is not influenced by Kyd's bombastic rhetoric. In fact he parodies a famous passage in Kyd's play, beginning "O eyes no eyes but fountains full of tears." The play was immensely popular at the time. The atrocities in the story have been made tolerable by being placed in ancient Rome.

Richard II

Topical relevance is a limiting factor in any work and Shakespeare's works are universal rather than topical. Yet the theme of this play was such that in the Elizabethan times it had topical relevance. Queen Elizabeth, seeing it, had angrily exclaimed: "I am Richard II, know ye that?... This tragedy is played forty times in open streets and houses." The king had divine rights, and his deposition was a highly sensitive issue. When the play was staged, all the scenes dealing with the deposition of King Richard II had to be omitted. It is thought that the play is a study in weakness of character in the person of the hero, Richard II.

A Midsummer Night's Dream

This charming comedy has been hailed as his best early comedy. It is a fantasy in which fairies take active part in the action and influence human beings. It has been claimed for Shakespeare that it was he who, in this play, created the new genre of fairy-tale comedy and he will use it again in his last play *The Tempest*. The art of characterisation is a special feature of this play, for three levels of characters have been presented in it: the fairies, the two pairs of romantic aristocratic lovers, and the robust earthy villagers. Bottom the weaver, of this last group, is the strongest portrayal and has passed into immortality.

Love's Labour's Lost

This play is notable for its dialogue of sparkling wit. He uses a host of courtly characters in it, all talking in highly polished language. Humbler characters are also present. A short passage of this play has become specially well-known. The merriest and wittiest of the lords, Lord Berowne, decides to give up ornate and witty diction ("taffeta phrases, silken terms precise") and adopt a simpler mode of speaking ("russet yeas and honest kersey noes."). Lord Berowne is supposed to be a slightly autobiographical character. The theme of love and marriage is treated here with great gusto and good-humour, the poet poking fun at the lords.

King John

This play contains a curious paradox in it. It is an entirely historical play yet it has topical relevance as well. In this play religion is an important issue, exactly as it was in those days. King John, just like Queen Elizabeth, carried on a lifelong struggle with the Pope. The focus of interest, however, is not religion, though it is an important issue. The play, therefore, cannot be called a religious play. It is, on the other hand, a historical play and essentially patriotic. The relationship with foreign powers is the central theme of the play, and this was one of the living issues of his own times as well.

The Merchant of Venice

This is the first of the group of the four romantic comedies, also known as the golden or the happy comedies. The merchant after whom the play is named is Antonio, yet he cannot be called the hero. The position of the most important character is taken by Shylock—a character who is a class by himself. The heroine Portia is one of the most important female characters of our poet. The Elizabethan stage-convention of disguise is used most effectively in the play, for all the three female characters in it adopt disguises. His poetic style has come to a high standard of excellence in it.

Henry IV, Parts 1 and 2

These two plays can be said to have taken the history play to a high peak of excellence not reached since then. Sir John

Falstaff has become the very epitome of a comic character.
Even Shakespeare's own later creation Sir Toby of *Twelfth
Night* pales by comparison. The play, though the comic scenes
steal the limelight, is about the serious issues of the duties of
and the responsibilities of kings. The second part of the play
emphasises the theme. This is seen the best in the rejection-
scene in which King Henry V rejects Falstaff. As Prince Hal he
had been a carefree young man, but when he becomes the king
he will have to bid farewell to his former life. So Falstaff is
rejected in one of the most moving scenes.

The Merry Wives of Windsor

Falstaff had so captivated Queen Elizabeth that she specially
ordered a play on "the fat knight in love." Thus this play
came to be written. This play begins at the point where *Henry
IV Pt. 2* ends. It is a boisterous farce, the only such play
Shakespeare had written. It is a simple, laughter-provoking
play, not a humorous satire. This is a feature to be noted
because one of the characters in it, Corporal Nym, is supposed
to be a parody of a humour character. By this time Ben Jonson
had started to write his highly successful humour comedies and
Nym is such a character.

King Henry V

Just as the three parts of *Henry VI*, together with *Richard
III*, make up a tetralogy, so do *Richard III*, the two *Henry IV*
parts and this play. King Henry V presents Shakespeare's
concept of the ideal king. The two dominant themes of the
play are those of patriotism and the duties of kingship. The
famous battle of Agincourt is presented in an entirely impartial
manner—with its heroism and nobility as well as its cruelty
and bloodshed. The young king is presented as the ideal leader
of men in the field of battle, but later when the battle comes
to an end he is the ideal king who knows how to temper
justice with mercy.

Much Ado About Nothing

This play is a romantic comedy and belongs to the group
of the golden or the happy comedies. Like all of them, this
play also revolves around the central theme of love. This theme

is presented in many different ways in this play. The Hero-Claudio plot gives physical love based on appearances, the Benedick-Beatrice plot presents the rejection of married love. The theme of love versus friendship is also presented as in *The Two Gentlemen of Verona*. Shakespeare's expertise in the management of plot is also evident, for there is a clear-cut main plot and another subsidiary plot. This clarity of outline is absent in *The Merchant of Venice*.

Julius Caesar

This is a Roman tragedy. The play is a purely political one and takes up the theme of the conflict between tyranny and liberty. The story is taken from Lord North's translation of Plutarch's *Lives*. It was highly successful on the stage. The Forum Scene with Mark Antony's famous speech is one of the highlights of the play. Shakespeare makes use of the supernatural element in the form of Julius Caesar's ghost. This is so important an element that scholars and critics have opined that Caesar's ghost casts a shadow over the entire play as the Ghost in *Hamlet* does.

As You Like It

This is avowedly the best of the golden comedies. More than half of the play is located in the pastoral environment of the forest of Arden and this has led to its being labelled as a pastoral comedy. Love, the central theme as in all romantic comedies, is presented in four different ways through four pairs of lovers. There are royal and courtly characters as well as humble shepherds. At the end of the play all are neatly paired off, with four marriages in the play. Rosalind is one of the most charming heroines and her use of a male disguise produces some effective examples of dramatic irony.

Twelfth Night

In this, the last of the golden comedies, the main theme is love and two different aspects of it have been dealt with. A later and paler counterpart of Falstaff is present in the person of Sir Toby. It also contains one of the most famous clowns of Shakespeare in the character of Feste. Shakespeare rarely used humour characters in his plays, but this play contains one such—Malvolio the melancholy Puritan. The heroine Viola, like the heroines of the three other golden comedies, adopts a male disguise and retains it for longer than any other heroine. The play takes up the theme of mistaken identities which was one of the first themes used by Shakespeare, in *The Comedy of Errors*. He has taken the story from many different sources.

Hamlet

This is the last of his plays written in the Elizabethan period. It is also the first of the group of the four great tragedies and ushers in a period of dark mood in Shakespeare's artistic career. It is basically a revenge tragedy, but the character of Hamlet has gained so much importance that this feature has receded into the background. Nothing can prove the supremacy of Shakespeare than the manner in which he has taken up the crude melodramatic form of the blood-and-thunder revenge tragedy and lifted it up to the heights of deep psychological complexity. It contains all the elements of a revenge tragedy, but soars up high beyond the limitations of one.

Troilus and Cressida

In this play Shakespeare goes far back in time and space for inspiration—to the world of Greek myths. This is the first of the problem comedies. These plays like the tragedies, deal with the problem of evil, but do not end tragically. The entire atmosphere is a dark and gloomy one and the plays are thus also known as the dark comedies. This play is thought to be Shakespeare's nearest approach to satire. There is a famous speech in the play, known as the degree speech, delivered by Ulysses who is a character known for his wisdom. It is thought that his speeches echo the thoughts of the dramatist himself.

All's Well that Ends Well

This play, like *Troilus and Cressida*, belongs to the group of problem comedies, but it is not so satirical as the former. The main plot, concerning Bertram and Helena, expounds the theme of the conflict between virtue and nobility. Apart from these there are many other sub-themes, like the hollowness of romantic love. Deception and mistaken identity are used as a basis for marriage. Rejection of devoted love is also one of the themes, for Bertram's rejection forces Helena to deceive him. The change in Shakespeare's attitude to life is seen most clearly in the figure of the satirical portrait of the braggart soldier, Parolles, who is totally different from the lovable Falstaff.

Measure for Measure

The third of the problem comedies, it is a very bitter play. The paradox is that this extremely gloomy comedy resembles *As You Like It*, the happiest of the happy comedies, in one respect—both end with no less than four marriages. Here also, as in *All's Well That Ends Well*, there is the theme of rejection of love. In addition there is the serious issue of justice and its administration, which is one of the important themes in his later plays. This also involves the social issues of morality and the law, and the religious issues of sin and grace. The seriousness of the poet's attitude is always in evidence.

Othello

This is the first of the tragedies performed in Jacobean times and is often called "the *Romeo and Juliet* of the later Shakespeare." It is also juxtaposed with the later Romance *The Winter's Tale*, as both the plays give us studies in jealousy. Othello, the hero presents the destructive effects of jealousy. There is also the figure of Iago which has puzzled the Shakespearean scholars because he brings about the tragic end by sowing the seeds of jealousy in Othello's mind for no discernible reason. Coleridge's famous phrase "motiveless malignity" describes Iago most aptly.

King Lear

This is his next work and the subject of the present book and can be by-passed.

Macbeth

This is taken to be Shakespeare's gloomiest play and is the fourth of the great tragedies. He has portrayed a Scottish hero as a compliment to King James. This can be classed as a Conqueror tragedy. This tragedy gives us the unique figure of Lady Macbeth, which is all the more remarkable as tragedies are hero-centred plays. She overshadows all but Macbeth. This play is also remarkable in that it makes use of the Three Witches whose prophecies are instrumental in bringing about the tragic end.

Antony and Cleopatra

This is classed as a Roman tragedy and depicts the events following *Julius Caesar*. As such it can be regarded as a sequel to it. It shows Mark Antony's life after the battle at Philippi. Caesar's empire was divided into three parts among the three members of the Triumvirate and Egypt had fallen to Mark Antony's share. He then goes to Egypt and meets Cleopatra. Thus the theme of love as an all-consuming and all-compensating factor is introduced. It is a historical tragedy on the theme of love and had inspired Dryden's *All for Love*.

Coriolanus

This too is classed, with *Julius Caesar* and *Antony and Cleopatra*, as a Roman tragedy. The theme of honour versus popularity is taken up here. The hero is a man of such nobility that he cannot stoop to make himself cheap in order to win popularity. This obstinacy brings about his tragic doom.

Timon of Athens

Classed among the problem comedies, this play had never been staged. It is now accepted by many scholars as an unfinished play, though at a superficial reading it seems to be a complete one. The last part of the play shows the misanthropic hero's withdrawal from society, and this gives the play some completeness.

Pericles

This is the first play of the last phase. He takes up the theme of sin and repentance which leads to forgiveness and to regeneration. This is the theme of all the last romances. It will recur, with variations, in all the last plays. All these plays have a rather unrealistic fairy-tale atmosphere which has led to their being grouped together as romances.

Cymbeline

This is the second play of the last group, treating the same theme as *Pericles*. Imogen, the heroine, dons a male disguise as the heroines of his earlier plays do. King Cymbeline, like Pericles, loses his children, but gets them back after long years of separation and repentance, as is the case with all the last romances.

The Winter's Tale

This play is often coupled with *Othello* as being a study in jealousy. In addition, it has all the other features of the last Romances. This play is well-known as being the most notorious violation of the classical rules of the Unities, particularly that of time, for it covers more than sixteen years. It contains some of the most charming pastoral scenes in Shakespeare. The theme of sin and repentance and forgiveness is to be found here as in all the last Romances. Leontes is one of his important male figures.

The Tempest

This is the last of the Romances and our poet's last play as well. It is thought that the figure of the wise Prospero is faintly autobiographical. The play was staged to celebrate a royal betrothal and it is thought that the poet himself acted in the role of Prospero. The same theme is taken up as in all the last romances and Miranda is a symbol of purity, innocence and virtue, more so than any other heroine.

Henry VIII

This play belongs to the cycle of chronicle plays, but it is different from them in that it discusses an important theme – patience in adversity. Not only the King but the other characters also have to learn this. The authorship of this play has for long been in doubt.

The Two Noble Kinsmen

This is a dramatisation of *The Knight's Tale* as told by Chaucer and was written in collaboration with Fletcher. The major parts of Act I, III and V were by Shakespeare. Then Fletcher introduced a vulgar sub-plot which was out of tune with the solemnity of the main plot concerning Palamon and Arcite. This displeased Shakespeare and he refused to collaborate any further with Fletcher.

REFERENCES

1. Ribner, Irving, *William Shakespeare: Life, Times and Theatre*. London: John Wiley & Sons Inc., 1969, p. 31.
2. Cited in Halliday, F.E., *The Life of Shakespeare*. London: Gerald Duckworth & Co. Ltd., 1961, p. 20.
3. Ribner, I., *op. cit.*, p. 38.
4. Halliday, F.E., *op. cit.*, p. 59.
5. Quoted in Ribner, *op. cit.*, p. 45.
6. Rowse, A.L., *William Shakespeare: A Biography*. London: Macmillan & Co. Ltd., 1963, p. 201.
7. Halliday, *op. cit.*, p. 118.
8. *Ibid.*, p. 138.
9. *Ibid.*, p. 183.
10. Quoted in Ribner, I., *op. cit.*, p. 64.

4

A Brief Outline and the Genre

(a) A Brief Outline of the Story

King Lear, more than any other play of Shakespeare, takes us back to the legendary times—times that were crude and violent, when anything and everything was possible. It does not deal with supernatural elements such as ghosts, spirits, witchery etc., yet the play is permeated with an atmosphere of other-worldliness and the reader has to suspend his disbelief, as Coleridge had said, willingly. It presents a dark world in which conventional values and moral concepts seem to fail.

King Lear, the old king ("fourscore and upwards"), has decided to withdraw from active administration. He has no sons but three daughters, two of whom are married. He decides to divide his kingdom among them.

It is here that the atmosphere of a fairy-tale world makes itself felt for Lear decides to test his daughters' love for him. A map is brought and he asks his daughters to proclaim their love for him. Goneril, the eldest is a sycophant and hypocrite and her answer pleases him. A third of the kingdom is given to her. The same happens with Regan who is as great a hypocrite as Goneril.

Next comes Cordelia's turn, the third and as yet unmarried daughter. The King loves her most and knows that she too is devoted to him. But this childish and undignified love-test distresses and repels her. So she answers Lear's eager questions with one word, "Nothing". Frustrated and angry, Lear disowns her and divides the rest of the kingdom between the two elder sisters.

The King of France and the Duke of Burgundy had both
come to pay court to Cordelia. The latter withdraws his suit.
The King of France, however, values her nobility and integrity
and happily takes her for his Queen:

> Fairest Cordelia, that art most rich, being poor;
> Thee and thy virtues here I seize upon:
> Be it lawful I take up what is cast away.[1]

The Earl of Kent protests against the injustice and is
banished from the kingdom. Lear decides to stay, with a
hundred attendant knights, with Goneril and Regan by turn,
one month with each.

The Earl of Gloucester, one of the important courtiers, is
the main character of the sub-plot. He has two sons, the
younger is illegitimate. This son Edmund, resents his illegitimacy
and is a consummate hypocrite. He is the villain of the play
just as Goneril and Regan are the two villainous characters in
the main plot. Edmund writes a letter in the name of Edgar,
Gloucester's legitimate son, purporting to conspire against his
father's life and shows it to Gloucester. Later he pretends to
have been attacked by Edgar. The Earl declares that Edgar is a
traitor and will be killed. The Duke of Cornwall (Regan's
husband) has come to stay in his castle and supports him.
Edgar goes into hiding.

Shakespeare now has two foolish fathers who have driven
away their devoted children from them and are now in the
hands of their cruel hypocritical children. The main and the
sub-plots thus parallel, and reinforce each other.

Goneril and Regan decide to neglect and defy their father
as much as they can. Lear has given away all his power and
wealth but does not realise this cruel truth, behaving as if he
were still the king. He hits Goneril's man for upbraiding his
Fool. Goneril, with whom he is staying first, decides to teach
him a lesson and tells her steward Oswald to behave insolently
to Lear.

Meanwhile, the loyal Duke of Kent comes in disguise to
Lear. He had been banished from the kingdom but he truly

loves Lear and comes hack in disguise to serve him. When Oswald comes and is rude to Lear, Kent punishes him.

Lear's Fool is one of the most remarkable Fools in Elizabethan and Jacobean drama. He sings and dances and entertains as a Fool is expected to do but he is remarkable in that he tries to instill some sense of his changed status into Lear's mind. Lear does not pay much attention to him and is taken aback when Goneril upbraids him, and asks him to reduce the number of his retinue. Lear at once decides to leave her and go to Regan. He curses Goneril in a terrible passage:

> Hear, Nature, hear! Dear goddess, hear!
> Suspend thy purpose, if thou didst intend
> To make this creature fruitful!
> Into her womb convey sterility.[2]

He comes to know that his retinue has been reduced to half its size by Goneril and, highly incensed, leaves for Regan's palace. Regan, however, has already been warned by Goneril, and though the Fool does not know of this, he is astute enough to guess Regan's possible reaction and tries to warn Lear. By this time Lear is afraid that his humiliations might make him mad and prays that he may keep his sanity.

After this there is steady downfall for Lear. Kent, who was bringing Lear's message to Regan, meets Oswald who was the bearer of Goneril's letter. The two of them fight and Kent is put in the stocks where he is found by Lear. When Lear succeeds in meeting Regan she, instead of blaming Goneril, supports her. Then Goneril herself arrives and the two sisters unite in insulting Lear. A storm is brewing and Lear, beside himself with rage and humiliation goes out in the impending storm with only the Fool for company.

Kent, who was out on a heath during this storm, meets a loyal Gentleman whom he sends to France to apprise Cordelia of the events at home. Lear enters the heath and Kent meets him. There is a hut nearby and Kent takes Lear and the Fool to this hut. By this time Lear is almost mad, but not fully. Edgar, disguised as a madman, is sheltering in the hut. So Shakespeare brings the Fool, the half-mad and the pretended madman together. Lear, in a significant speech, prays for all the poor and destitute men of his kingdom.

Edmund, meanwhile, has persuaded the Duke of Cornwall that the Earl of Gloucester has betrayed him. Gloucester, unaware of all this, tries to help King Lear by taking him to a farmhouse attached to his castle. This gives Cornwall proof of his supposed treachery. He also receives information that the King of France has landed with his army and this only confirms Gloucester's guilt. He has the latter arrested and puts out his eyes and thrusts him out of his own house. A servant of the Earl, unable to bear this injustice, follows him to comfort and guide him. One of his servants, in protest, had fought Cornwall and seriously injured him.

Gloucester, blind, reaches the place in the heath where Edgar is. Edgar, still pretending to be mad, leads him to Dover. Blindness has opened the inner eyes of his father and he now realises what an injustice he had done to Edgar. He wants to atone for this sin and means to commit suicide, though this is not made at all clear at this stage of the play.

Edmund has won the earldom of his father and now Goneril is in love with him. Albany, her husband, had supported her up till now. But at this point he turns against her for her inhumanity, though he does not know about her infidelity. While he is in this mood a message comes from Cornwall, bringing the news of Gloucester's blinding and Cornwall's death.

The King of France and Cordelia had landed with their army at Dover. King Lear is entirely mad by now and is roving about in the fields. While Cordelia sends out a search-party for him she is told of the advance of the British army.

Edgar brings his father to a place in Dover and convinces him that he is standing on a cliff. Gloucester then, wishing to commit suicide, throws himself down. Edgar, appearing like a peasant, persuades him that he had truly jumped from a high cliff and is alive only by God's mercy. While they are talking Lear comes to them. Gloucester, though blind, recognises him by his voice. It is here that Oswald sees Gloucester and tries to kill him but is himself killed by Edgar. Goneril's love-letter to Edmund, which Oswald was going to deliver, now comes to Edgar which he keeps for future use.

Lear is finally united to Cordelia. He is now in his right mind and it is a blissful union. They, however, are fated not to be left in peace, for there is a battle and Cordelia's army is defeated. She along with Lear, is taken prisoner, and they go gladly to prison.

It is Edmund who was leading the victorious army. Regan, who is a widow and therefore free to remarry, now publicly proclaims that she takes him as her husband. Goneril cannot bear this and the two sisters quarrel publicly over him. Albany now proclaims him a traitor and challenges him to prove his innocence. A formal proclamation is made by a herald, inviting any warrior to come and fight Edmund. This proclamation is heard by Edgar and he, dressed for battle, answers the challenge. Before doing so he had finally revealed his identity to his father. The Earl of Gloucester, after blessing him, died peacefully.

The two brothers fight and Edmund is defeated. At his defeat Goneril is mortified. She takes the terrible step of poisoning her sister and then kills herself—a miserable end for a despicable woman.

Edmund, on seeing their dead bodies, is overcome with remorse. He tries to revoke his order to· kill King Lear and Cordelia, with which work he had entrusted an officer of the army. The harm has already been done and Cordelia has been hanged. Lear carries in her dead body, and all the while under the illusion that she still breathes, dies.

Now the main characters, good as well as evil, are dead. The crown of Britain comes to Albany. It is his sacred duty now to restore order in the kingdom and rule it wisely. He proclaims:

> All friends shall taste
> The wages of their virtue, and all foes
> The cups of their deserving.[3]

Thus, with the restoration of moral order, as is necessary at the end of a tragedy, the play comes to an end.

(b) The Genre of the Play

As it is, *King Lear*, along with *Hamlet*, *Othello* and *Macbeth*, is definitely categorized as one of the four Great Tragedies, yet there are other opinions about it also. Many critics have found other elements in it and have called it by other names. Some of these shall be explained now.

A Pathetic Tragedy

This is one of the earliest opinions and it is given by the famous actor-director of the eighteenth century, David Garrick. This is the view of G.W. Stone. According to him Garrick saw the play as a:

> Shakespearean play which could
> surpass competition from all writers of
> pathetic tragedy and could command the
> emotional pleasures of tears more suc-
> cessfully than sentimental comedy.[4]

The term "pathetic tragedy" as given here is not an ordinary epithet but "pathetic tragedy" is a special kind of tragedy. Aristotle divided tragedies into four categories of which pathetic tragedy is one:

> There are four kinds of tragedies, the complex, depending
> entirely on Reversal of the Situation and Recognition, the
> pathetic (where the motive is passion)....[5]

Aristotle does not explain the nature of pathetic tragedy any further though later commentators have tried to elaborate the concept. It is important for us to note here that everyone agrees that *King Lear* portrays violent passions

Coleridge: He is the open and ample play-room of nature's passions.

Lamb: The explosions of his passion are as terrible as a volcano.

Keats:　　　　The fierce dispute
Betwixt damnation and impassioned clay
Must I burn through.[6]

These are a few of the early opinions but these are impressions with which everyone agrees. Aristotle had emphatically expressed this aspect of the pathetic tragedy—it is a tragedy which explores human passions, and their expressions are most spectacular—particularly those of Lear. Those of the other characters also are not neglected. Thus in Edmund the malcontent we have the passions of jealousy and ambition. Goneril and Regan both exhibit adulterous passion for Edmund which brings about murder and suicide. All the actions that take place in the play, all the events that occur, are the direct or indirect results of different passions motivating the different characters.

As a Romance

It has been averred that the story and the plot of *King Lear* is more befitting to a romance than a tragedy. The story of the love-test, for example, does not have anything realistic about it. As the play progresses unreal and improbable events are heaped upon one another. Maynard Mack gives a list of all those features that differentiate this play from the other Shakespearean tragedies:

1. In this play alone among the tragedies we are asked to take seriously literal disguises that deceive.
2. This is the only Shakespearean tragedy in which a number of the characters are conceived in terms of unmitigated goodness and badness.
3. The only one where the plot is made up of incidents each more incredible—naturalistically, than the last.[7]

The disguises adopted in this play are three (For more information on this head see Chapter 9, *Plot, infra*). The Earl of Kent disguises himself as Caius and Edgar disguises himself as a madman first and as a peasant next. The disguises, in all three cases, are so successful that they deceive even those who bear a very near and intimate relationship. Kent is a trusted follower of the King, but when he comes to Lear as Caius no one can recognise him. Cordelia recognises him only after he has revealed his identity to her. Later he reveals himself to

Edgar who then makes him known to the others. This happens only in the last scene.

Edgar's disguise taxes the audience's credulousness even further, for his own father does not recognise him. It is true that Gloucester is blind, but it is surprising that he does not recognise his own son's voice. It is not that he cannot recognise any voice at all, for when he comes across Lear in his madness, he recognises the King by his voice:

> The trick of that voice I do well remember:
> Is it not the King?[8]

He can identify the King by his voice, but not his son.

The other features that Maynard Mack gives are also easily understood. Taking the second point, Goneril, Regan, Cornwall and Edmund are evil characters and Cordelia, Kent, Gloucester and Edgar are the good ones. The incidents that take place in the play (his third point) are truly, each of them, unnatural or, as the critic calls them, naturalistically incredible. He then comes to the conclusion:

> This is the heady brew of romance, not tragedy.[9]

Romance deals with the unnatural, the incredible and the unrealistic. The study of *King Lear* does, indeed, create an other-worldly atmosphere in which anything may happen, as in romance.

As a Grotesque Comedy

In a famous essay, G. Wilson Knight points out that the heart-rending tragedy of King Lear often approaches the level of grotesque comedy. According to him the play is a mass of incongruities and improbabilities. These are the features of comedy, not of tragedy:

> The course of the action often comes as near to the resolution of comedy as of tragedy.[10]

He then goes on to analyse the play from this point of view and finds elements of comedy everywhere. For example Lear's love-test in the beginning of the play is a childish and foolish trick inviting deception. Wilson Knight remarks:

> The incident is profoundly comic and profoundly pathetic.[11]

He finds this comic element in each incident and even in each character. Lear has a "tremendous soul" but "a puerile intellect" which is an incongruity that gives rise to grotesque comedy. The Fool is continually pointing out this feature:

> The Fool is used as a chorus, pointing to us the absurdity of the situation.... He is not all wrong when he treats the situation as matter for a jest.[12]

The storm-scenes focus on this element of the incongruous, repeatedly highlighting the comic aspect of the situation and so does the mock trial-scene. Wilson Knight quotes Gloucester's famous lines as the key to the mood of the play:

> As flies to wanton boys are we to the gods
> They kill us for their sport.[13]

A little boy will laugh at the tortured writings of an impaled insect and this, according to the critic, explains the prevailing mood of the play:

> We are clearly pointed to this grim fun, this hideous sense of humour, at the back of tragedy.[14]

A Christian Allegory

This is the view of many critics. They are all overawed by the sight of Lear's sufferings which seem to have no end, and have a religious aura. Suffering, according to Christianity and, indeed, according to many other religions, is a necessary step to salvation and Lear's sufferings have a cosmic dimension. This is because they are so manifestly out of proportion to his guilt. He is guilty of foolishness and arrogance, but his sufferings are much too terrible for him and, indeed, for anybody. Cordelia also is a figure of undeserved suffering. She is the very soul of goodness and she has not done anything to offend the gods. Yet she is separated from her beloved father, her native land, imprisoned and finally killed ignominiously. There are many critics who see a religious significance in all this:

R.W. Chambers: *King Lear* is like the *Paradiso,* a vast poem on the victory of true love.

J.F. Danby: *King Lear* is at least as Christian as the *Divine Comedy.*

G. Beckersteth: Divine Love, symbolised by Cordelia, enters a kingdom already divided against itself, which is the Christian definition of Hell.[15]

This is a very serious interpretation, involving as it does a religious outlook. It argues that the play shows the sufferings of the King as a punishment for his *hybris* (*Vide* Chapter 7, *infra* for an explanation of this term). This suffering purges him of all the imperfections in his character and finally he emerges as a morally and spiritually elevated character. He is likened to Christ, and the play is looked upon as an allegory or a morality play.

King Lear has been interpreted in many other ways,—a play of intrigue, a folk-tale, a morality. Such widely divergent opinions go to prove the complexity and the immensity of the play. All are partially true, but none succeeds in fully explaining it.

REFERENCES

1. Muir, Kenneth, ed., The Arden ed of *King Lear*, Univ. Pbks, London, Methuen, 1980. Act I, sc.i, lines 249-51, p. 19. All future references to the text are to this edition.

2. Act I, sc.iv, lines 273-76, p. 48.

3. Act V, sc.iii, lines 301-03, p. 204.

4. Mack, Maynard, *Actors and Redactors*, in Kermode, F., ed., *King Lear : A Case-Book*. London: Macmillan 1978 rpt., p. 59.

5. Butcher, S.H., *Aristotle's Theory of Poetry and Fine Arts with a Critical Text Translation of 'The Poetics'*. New Delhi: Kalyani Pubs., 1981, pp. 65-67.

6. Kermode, F., *op. cit.*, pp. 39, 44, 45.

7. Mack, M., *op. cit.*, p. 52.

8. Act IV, sc.vi, lines 106-7, pp. 164-65.

9. Mack, M., *op. cit.*, p. 52.

10. Knight, G. Wilson, *King Lear and the Comedy of the Grotesque*, in Kermode, F., *op. cit.*, p. 119.

11. *Ibid.*

12. *Ibid.*, p. 121.

13. Act IV, sc.i, lines 36-7, p. 140.

14. Knight, *op. cit.*, p. 129.

15. Chambers, R.W., *King Lear*, Danby, J.F., *Shakespeare's Doctrine of Nature*, Beckersteth, *The Golden World of King Lear*. All quoted by Everett, B., in *The New King Lear*, in Kermode, F., *op. cit.*, p. 191.

5

A Scene-wise Analysis

Act I, sc. i

In this, the first scene of the play, we see the Earl of Kent and the Earl of Gloucester with his son. They are discussing the vexatious question of the division of the kingdom. They make it clear that the King's attitude towards his two sons-in-law, the Duke of Albany (the husband of Goneril), and the Duke of Cornwall (the husband of Regan) is totally impartial.

Kent then asks Gloucester whether Edmund is his son or not, and the latter discloses the fact that Edmund is his younger and illegitimate son and introduces him to Kent. After this King Lear enters with his retinue and the real business of the play begins.

This part of the scene, covering about thirty-two lines, is in prose. It is in the nature of a Prologue (*Vide* Chapter 9, *Plot*, *infra* for more information). In the plays of this time, the prologue is very often not given independently but is part of the first scene. In this play, the dramatist has skillfully separated the prologue from the main action by writing it in prose. The rest of the scene, except for the last part, is in verse.

This part of the scene introduces two characters of the sub-plot, the Earl of Gloucester and Edmund. Kent is going to play an important part in the main plot, so he too is introduced here.

King Lear enters with his three daughters and two sons-in-law. He gets the map of Britain unfolded and tells everyone his intention of dividing the kingdom according to how much

each daughter loves him. Goneril speaks in extravagant terms
of her love for him. Her manifest hypocrisy disgusts Cordelia
and she says aside:

What shall Cordelia speak? Love and be silent.[1]

Lear is very pleased with Goneril and allots a part of the
kingdom to her and then turns to Regan. She does not lag
behind and overwhelms him with the protestation of the
strength of her love. Here again Cordelia reveals herself in a
scornful aside. Then comes her own turn.

She is so disgusted by the whole affair that she refuses to
speak. This is not at all surprising, for no self-respecting person
would like to make a public exhibition of his or her love. The
dialogue runs thus:

Cordelia: Nothing, my lord.

Lear: Nothing?

Cordelia: Nothing.

Lear: Nothing will come of nothing: speak again.

Cordelia: Unhappy that I am, I cannot heave
           My heart into my mouth: I love your majesty
           According to my bond; no more, nor less.[2]

Nothing moves her and she holds her stand in spite of all that
Lear can say. He even appeals to her feelings:

Lear: But goes thy heart with this?

Cordelia: Ay, my good Lord.

Lear: So young and so untender?

Cordelia: So young, my Lord, and true.[3]

Then Lear becomes angry and disowns her. He divides the
rest of the kingdom between Goneril and Regan. He tells them
that they will get all the revenues, and he will not keep
anything for himself. He will only have a retinue of a hundred
knights and spend one month each, alternately, with his two
elder daughters. He shall keep the designation of "King", but
resign all the wealth and the power of the kingdom. He is
bitterly disappointed in Cordelia for he had thought that after
giving her portion of the kingdom he would spend the rest of

his life with her. Now that has become impossible due, as he thinks, to her obstinacy.

At this point the Earl of Kent tries to intervene. He tells the King not to be so unwise. His plain words only inflame Lear and he is banished.

Now the Duke of Burgundy and the King of France come on the stage and Lear clarifies Cordelia's position to them. The Duke of Burgundy has a mercenary motive and withdraws his suit, for he does not want a dowerless wife. The King of France is truly noble and appreciates Cordelia's integrity:

> Gods, gods! 'tis strange that from their cold'st neglect
> My love should kindle to inflam'd respect
> Thy dowerless daughter, King, thrown to my chance
> Is Queen of us, of ours, and our fair France.[4]

Lear goes away with his court and only the King of France and Cordelia linger in order to bid farewell to the two sisters. This done, they too go and the two elder sisters are alone on the stage.

Here follows a dialogue in prose. The two sisters agree with each other that Lear is a foolish man and does not know his own nature. They criticise him freely and it becomes quite clear that they have no love or reverence for him and will neglect and humiliate him at the first chance. The audience's fear that they are both hypocrites is seen to be true.

Shakespeare's scenes are usually interconnected. This is the first scene, so it provides the basis on which the others will be built. Indeed, this foolish action of Lear is the seed from which the entire scene is going to spread its branches. So it is integrally connected with the following scenes.

The scene also has a fairy-tale atmosphere. In fact there are several fairy tales in which a foolish king heckles his daughters on how much they love him and he is deceived by them. A sense of unreality is thus noticeable in this first scene. Shakespeare has also condensed seven scenes of his source-play into this one scene (*Vide* Chapter 9 *Plot, infra*). Because of all these reasons the first scene has been thought to be a failure. Allardyce Nicoll says:

Shakespeare has left us with something which simply cannot be tolerated on the stage, for, to find an explanation of Lear's decision and demeanour in this first scene we need to know the subsequent development of the play.[5]

From the point of view of construction, the scene has been extremely well-planned. It is distinctly divisible into three parts. The first part, consisting of the dialogue between Kent, Edmund and his father, comes to thirty-two lines and is written in prose. The middle part, from line no. 33 to 281 is in poetry and contains the most important events. Then comes the third part, from line no. 282 to 307, nearly twenty-five lines, in prose. The middle part stands out from the rest, for it is written in poetry and contains the most important events of the play. It is a long scene, but not the longest in the play. In fact it shares the honour of being the third longest scene of this play with the fourth scene of Act II, both having 307 lines.

Act I, sc. ii

This scene reveals the true colour of Edmund, the illegitimate son of the Duke of Gloucester. He bitterly resents the fact that he is illegitimate and yet is shrewd enough to cover his resentment under a cloak of hypocrisy. He has written a letter in Edgar's name, purporting to hatch a conspiracy to kill their father. He pretends to hide this letter in such a manner as to rouse the Duke's suspicions. He naturally insists on seeing the letter and thinks it to be proof enough of Edgar's treachery. It does not cross his mind that the letter may be a forgery. He tells Edmund to contact Edgar so that he may talk to him and know his true nature, and his true intentions.

It so happens that, almost as soon as Gloucester goes away, Edgar comes in. Edmund then tells him that their father is extremely angry with him and he must hide till the Duke is in a better mood. The scene ends with a clear revelation of Edmund's mind:

> Let me, if not by birth, have lands by wit:
> All with me is meet that I can fashion fit.[6]

These lines make up a couplet. Seneca, who exercised great

influence on the English writers of this time, gives such couplets to highlight moral lesson and they are known as "sententiae." Shakespeare, too, makes use of this technique, usually at the end of Acts and scenes, but not always to pinpoint morals. His couplets usually sum up the theme and often, as here, are used to reveal the mental state of the speaker. This scene is important mainly because it reveals Edmund as a malcontent and a Machiavellian plotter.

Act I, sc. iii

This scene, though short, is important because it lays the foundations for Lear's humiliation later. Here Goneril is talking to Oswald, her steward. A gentleman of her court had upbraided Lear's Fool for some reason and the King had then struck this man. Goneril is very resentful and complains of Lear's own behaviour as well as of his knights. She tells her steward and other servants to be rude to and neglect Lear. She knows that if he goes to Regan he will meet with no better treatment. Goneril is so resentful because Lear still behaves as if he were the King:

> Idle old man,
> That still would manage those authorities
> That he hath given away.[7]

Empson, referring to this scene and the incident of Lear's striking Goneril's man for having chid the Fool, points out:

> So it is the Fool who causes the beginning of the storm against Lear, rather than his shadowy train of debased knights.[8]

Act I, sc. iv

This is the longest scene of the play, containing three hundred and forty-seven lines. We see the Earl of Kent here. He had been banished for having protested against the injustice done to Cordelia. He is a loyal and devoted subject of King Lear and has now come back after having disguised himself, to serve the King. He has misgivings about the attitude of Goneril and Regan and knows that now that the King has given away all his power, he will need loyal persons to protect him. When the King comes Kent introduces himself as one named Caius who wants to serve him. Lear accepts him provisionally, subject to whether he likes him or not.

Oswald comes, and when Lear asks him where Goneril is, goes away without answering him. Then one of his knights tells him that she as well as her servants have become rude and careless in their behaviour.

Now Lear wants his Fool and we are told how the Fool has "pined away" since Cordelia's departure.

Then Oswald comes and speaks rudely, for which Kent beats him. Immediately after this the Fool enters. He is one of the most important characters in the play. He is Lear's court-jester and though called the Fool is actually a far wiser man than Lear himself. He tries, again and again throughout the play, to open Lear's eyes to the injustice he had done to Cordelia and also to his present situation:

Why, this fellow has banished two on's daughters and did the third a blessing against his will.[9]

Then he sings a song in which he calls Lear a fool:

Lear: Dost thou call me a fool, boy?

Fool: All thy other titles thou hast given away; that thou wast born with.[10]

Finally Goneril comes and delivers a diatribe against Lear's retinue and then asks him to reduce their number. Lear has by now realised her attitude and decides to go to Regan. Bitter remorse assails him and along with this there is rage in his heart.

He curses Goneril, invoking the Goddess Nature to make her barren or give her an unnatural child that she may feel:

How sharper than a serpent's tooth it is
To have a thankless child.[11]

Albany, her husband, had come in and he was in complete ignorance about Goneril's doings. Before he can do anything Lear discovers that fifty of his knights have been dismissed. Once more he curses Goneril and then leaves her—for Regan.

Goneril tells Oswald to take her letter to Regan, informing her of everything. Albany tries to restrain her but she merely scoffs at him. Albany utters a warning but he shows himself to be a rather weak person, for he gives in to her.

This is the longest scene in the play and one of the most important ones. It is linked to the earlier scenes, particularly the first, in that it is a direct result of that scene. It also looks forward to the next scene in that the King is going to Regan's Castle.

The scene has great variety in that it contains dialogues in prose as well as poetry and no less than five songs. It marks a turning-point in the play in that Lear's fortunes will be going downhill from now on. The appearance of Kent is significant for he will be the one to accompany Lear in his misfortunes, and send the news to Cordelia. He is also the first character in the play to adopt a disguise.

Act I, sc. v

This is the last scene of this Act. It serves as a connecting link between the foregoing scene and the next Act in that in it Lear sends Kent with a letter to Regan to apprise her of his coming. He is quite sure of his welcome, but the Fool has misgivings. He tries to warn Lear that Regan may behave just like Goneril, but Lear is too taken up with Goneril's behaviour to pay serious attention to him. Lear is afraid that the great tension may upset his reason:

> O! let me not be mad, not mad, sweet heaven;
> Keep me in temper; I would not be mad.[12]

This prepares us for the eventual loss of his reason.

This scene is mainly in prose, except for the two lines quoted above and a Senecan couplet spoken by the Fool at the end. The first Act ends with this.

The first Act, thus, has introduced all the characters to us and the action of both plots has progressed. We have seen King Lear at the height of his powers, dividing his kingdom most unwisely. Then because of this foolish act, his downfall starts. As the play proceeds, Shakespeare will gradually divest

him of all royal attributes and take away even his reason. The
characters of Goneril, Albany and the wise Fool have also been
sketched in. In the sub-plot there is Gloucester, as foolish a
father as Lear, has driven away his loyal son, trusting Edmund
who is a malcontent as well as the villain of the play.

Act II, sc. i

We now come to the castle of the Earl of Gloucester.
Edmund comes to know that the Duke of Cornwall and
Regan will be arriving that very night and so he weaves a plot.
He calls Edgar whom he had hidden in his room and tells him
to leave the place as soon as possible, because their father has
come to know his whereabouts.

The minute that Edgar goes away he pretends as if he had
been fighting Edgar and has been wounded. His father comes
and, hearing all this, becomes even more angry with Edgar.
While they are talking the Duke of Cornwall and Regan arrive.
On hearing of all this, they sympathise with father and son
and assure them that Edgar will not be allowed to escape and
will be punished as a traitor.

This scene, too, is written in a mixture of prose and verse,
for at the start of it Edmund and Curan who is a courtier talk
in prose and then after Edgar enters the rest of the scene is in
verse. It shows Edmund's quick-wittedness as well as his
wickedness. Hypocrisy and quick-wittedness are two of the
most well-known features of a malcontent. The sub-plot, thus,
is taken a step furthur in this scene. Yet the scene is not totally
isolated from the main plot, for two of the characters of the
main plot, the Duke of Cornwall and Regan his wife, are
present in it. The manner in which Edmund makes use of the
unforeseen opportunity afforded by Cornwall and Regan is
truly admirable.

Act II, sc. ii

This scene, too, is located, as the previous one, in the castle
of the Earl of Gloucester. The difference is that the foregoing
scene took place in a courtyard within the castle and this scene
is outside it. Kent and Oswald meet, insult each other and
fight. While they are fighting Edmund, Cornwall, Regan and

the Earl enter. The two are separated and Kent introduces himself as Lear's follower. This only puts Regan and her husband against him and they put him in the stocks. When they all go away we come to know from Kent's soliloquy that Cordelia has written to him. This raises the hope that, since she is in regular contact with him, she will come to know about Lear's condition and come to rescue him.

Act II, sc. iii

This is a very short scene and presents Edgar, delivering a soliloquy. He is now a hunted man and has escaped the search party by hiding in a forest. All the ports are being watched so he cannot leave the country. He decides to adopt a disguise— that of a madman, Poor Tom. He is going to be one of the companions of King Lear in the storm-scenes and this disguise will help.

This is one of the shortest scenes, being of only twenty-one lines. It is connected with the main body of the play, for it looks back to the first scene of this Act and forward to the storm-scenes. It also gives us the second disguise adopted in the play.

Act II, sc. iv

This scene begins with Lear's arrival at Gloucester's castle. He is outraged at seeing Kent in the stocks, as it is an insult to himself. He is told that Regan and her husband are not ready to meet him. While he is trying to adjust himself to this insult, they come on the stage. Kent is set free. When Lear appeals to Regan for sympathy he is told that it is he who is in the wrong. Regan tells him to go and apologise to Goneril. Lear once more curses Goneril and hardly has he stopped speaking than she herself arrives. Regan welcomes her and tells Lear to go and stay with her, for she is not yet ready to receive him and his retinue. The two sisters then vie with each other in insulting him. Goneril had reduced his retinue of a hundred knights to fifty and Regan is not ready to provide for even this reduced number. She tells him to keep only twenty-five, and finally asks why should he need even one. Then comes one of the most famous passages of the play. These evidences of his daughters' ingratitude almost unseat his reason but as yet he is still not insane.

In the midst of his speech a storm is heard in the distance and the King goes out in the impending storm. The Earl of Gloucester and the Fool accompany him. A few minutes later the former returns. He seeks to wring some sympathy out of the unnatural daughters but they merely tell him to close the doors of the castle and forbid him to help Lear.

This is one of the cruellest scenes in the play. It is true that a much worse fate is going to befall the King but he comes to know for the first time that there is no hope of succour for him. He has no one to turn to and his humiliation is complete. He still has his royal nobility and self-respect for, rather than stay with these daughters, he goes out in the storm.

The two daughters and Cornwall are shown as monsters of cruelty and ingratitude. This, however, is not the worst. Shakespeare is yet to sound the lowest depth of human nature in these characters.

The scene is written in prose as well as in verse, for the Fool talks in prose and sings some songs as well. The songs here as well as in the other scenes are full of hidden, satirical meanings, commenting on the prevailing situation.

It is also the last scene of the Act. Both the main as well as the sub-plots have made significant progress. Lear's punishment for his arrogant foolishness has already started, but Gloucester's is yet to come. Edgar is discredited and brought to a negation of his own identity. Kent has already given up his identity. Shakespeare is slowly bringing the main plot and the sub-plot together not only in theme but in other respects as well, because Edgar, all unawares is prepared to be a fit companion to the King in his misfortune. It also prepares us for the central scenes, known as the heath-scenes or the storm-scenes. This scene thus, like the others, looks backward to the foregoing scenes and forward to the following ones.

Act III, sc. i

Here we see Kent and a certain Gentleman out on the heath. Kent has not yet seen the King and he asks the Gentleman if he knows anything about him. The Gentleman, in answer tells how the King is raging about, bare-headed, in this inclement weather, with none but the Fool to keep him company. Kent sees that he is sympathetic towards the King and trusts him with a message for Cordelia. He also gives his ring to give to Cordelia and some money for the journey. This short scene prepares us for the coming of Cordelia.

Act III, sc. ii

This is one of the famous storm-scenes. We see the King out on the heath where a storm is raging. This is the storm that was impending in the last-scene of Act II and now we are in the midst of it.

The scene opens with Lear's invocation to the elements. However, destructive they might be, they are not as terrible as his daughters:

> I tax you not, you elements, with unkindness;
> I never gave you kingdom, called you children,
> You owe me no subscription.[13]

The Fool continually tries to distract his attention by jesting and singing, but Lear pays him but scant attention. Then Kent enters but the King hardly notices him. It is here that he speaks a short sentence that has gained, like many of Shakespeare's lines, the status of a proverb:

> I am a man
> More sinn'd against than sinning.[14]

Kent tries to take him to a hut nearby but Lear does not pay attention at first. Then he becomes aware that there are others who are suffering and shows consideration for them:

> How dost, my boy? Art cold?
> I am cold myself, where is this straw, my fellow?[15]

The Fool sings four lines and then after Lear has gone out with Kent he speaks a few couplets which he calls a prophecy (*Vide* Chapter 11, sec.(b), *infra*). At first it gives a description

of the real state of things and then it refers to an ideal future
and also describes himself as being more ancient than Merlin.

This is the first of the storm-scenes. The next scene but one
also takes place in the open heath, though they are standing
outside a hut in that scene. The King, half-crazed by anger and
grief, is still in his right mind and shows consideration for the
poor Fool who is getting drenched. This feature will be
heightened in the later scene which this one looks forward to.
This scene contains great variety of style in that we have blank
verse, prose, couplets as well as songs. This is the fourth scene
of this Act, presenting a situation almost unparalleled in the
depiction of terrible and undeserved suffering. The prison-
scene in Webster's *The Duchess of Malfi* is the only parallel to
these scenes.

Act III, sc. iii

In this short scene we see the Earl of Gloucester with the
villainous Edmund, trustfully confiding in him the fact that
Duke of Cornwall and Regan (who are his masters) have
imposed their rule on his house and told him never to plead
for Lear. He further confides that he has received a letter
apprising of the French invasion which will avenge Lear's
wrongs. He decides that he will look after the King even if he
dies for it. As soon as he goes Edmund tells us that he is going
to inform Cornwall of Gloucester's disobedience.

This scene looks forward to the seventh scene of this Act,
in which Gloucester, blinded, is driven out. It comes after four
more scenes after this one, but the link is established here. This
scene, like many others, uses both verse and prose, for Gloucester's
speech is in prose and Edmund speaks five lines in verse.

Act III, sc. iv

This is another storm-scene but at least the King is near a
shelter here. He is much calmer now, for the first fury of his
passion has spent itself. Kent pleads with him to enter the hut.
He replies:

> This tempest in my mind
> Doth from my senses take all feelings else
> Save what beats there—filial ingratitude.[16]

Now, however, he is fast approaching a state of grace. He makes the Fool enter the hut and then, still standing outside in the storm and darkness, he prays for all poor people in one of the most famous passages:

> Poor naked wretches, wheresoe'r you are,
> That bide the pelting of this pitiless storm,
> How shall your houseless heads and unfed sides,
> Your loop'd and window'd raggedness defend you
> From seasons such as these? O! I have ta'en
> Too little care of this. Take physic, Pomp;
> Expose thyself to feel what wretches feel,
> That thou mayst shake the superflux to them
> And show the Heavens more just.[17]

This is a crucial passage as it shows the King travelling through suffering towards a more mature and selfless outlook. He had never given a thought to the poor and now his eyes have been opened. He is thinking of those who have not got the bare necessities of life.

After this noble and ennobling prayer they encounter Edgar, disguised as Poor Tom the madman. He had decided to adopt this disguise in the third scene of Act II and thus the two scenes become linked together (*Vide* the analysis of Act II, sc. iii, *supra*). The question that Lear puts to him is very significant:

> Didst thou give all to thy daughters
> And art thou come to this?[18]

This makes us wonder whether he is entirely in his right mind. Empson is of the opinion that he is already mad, though all the Shakespearean critics do not think so:

Madness has come.—No doubt the appearance of Edgar...is the accident that made him unable to shun it any more.[19]

Edgar's prose speech is supposed to be a madman's nonsense but is full of many references and allusions. Looking at him, Lear is struck by the wretchedness of man's condition and feels it would be better to take off all his clothes so he could be nearer to Tom who is wearing only a blanket.

Gloucester enters with a torch and is shocked to see that the King has only Kent, the Fool and a madman for company. Kent tells him that the King is nearly mad, and in return Gloucester tells him of the supposed ingratitude of his son (Edgar) which has made him too almost mad. He, however, succeeds in making the King enter the hut. The entire scene takes place outside the hut. Things can hardly be worse, but the worst is still to come, for Lear is not yet entirely mad, and Gloucester is still in possession of his eyes and his property.

As far as the style is concerned, this scene has great variety for it has poetry, prose and song. Usually it is the Fool who sings but in this scene he is quiet and it is Edgar who sings. He sings four times, but the songs are not complete ones. This is but fitting for he is no singer but a madman. He recognises his father, but Gloucester does not recognise him. In mood and atmosphere this scene is almost a duplicate of the former storm-scene, except for the fact that Lear's character shows more development in this one.

Act III, sc. v

In this scene we see Edmund acquainting the Duke of Cornwall with the supposed treachery of his father. Cornwall at once decides to imprison the Earl and take away his title. He tells Edmund that it is he who is the Earl of Gloucester now. Edmund is elated and now only one more thing is needed to make his triumph complete:

If I find him comforting the King, it will stuff his suspicions more fully.[20]

This is a very short scene, consisting of only twenty-four lines, and is entirely in prose. Its function is to show how one more nail is hammered into Gloucester's coffin. Edmund's evil nature is intensified.

Act III, sc. vi

Here Gloucester takes the King's party to a farmhouse near his castle and leaves them there. Thereafter there is a conversation between the King, the Fool and Edgar. Kent takes but little part in it. It is the well-known and mock trial-scene.

Lear is half-mad and imagines that he is judging Goneril and Regan in a court. He addresses Edgar and the Fool as judges and Kent is also told to sit with them. Lear himself is the plaintiff. Goneril and Regan, the accused, are, of course, absent, but Lear imagines them to be present. The trial begins, but it cannot continue for long because soon enough Lear thinks that Goneril and Regan have run away. He is almost entirely mad and thinks that his own dogs are barking at him. He goes to sleep, remarking that he will have supper in the morning and the Fool remarks: "And I'll go to bed at noon." This is the last sentence spoken by him, and can be interpreted in seven different ways.

Gloucester has made arrangements for Lear to be conveyed to Dover where the French army is encamped. They take the King away in a litter, leaving Edgar on the stage. There is a soliloquy by him, in couplets, except for the last two lines.

This scene, like the other long scenes, has great variety of style. There is prose, spoken mainly by Edgar, poetry (spoken by the King, Kent and Gloucester), couplets (spoken by Edgar at the end) and three songs (one sung by the Fool and two by Edgar). Apart from the pity and terror with which the figure of King Lear inspires us, there is also the element of madness. Lear is fully mad now and Edgar, comparing his own state with that of Lear, finds that he is the one who is better off. A madman is beyond all moral and religious judgements and Lear, as a tragic hero has now gone beyond ordinary human conventions—social, ethical or religious. Yet, all unawares, he inspires fortitude in Edgar. Shakespeare has made him pass through the fire of suffering so that he may be brought to stop thinking of and pitying himself and think of other poor people. This madness will totally purify him.

Act III, sc. vii

This is the last scene of this Act and Shakespeare makes us witness another horrible atrocity in it. The Duke of Cornwall has had Gloucester arrested. He also receives the news that the French army has landed at Dover, where a few loyal knights have taken King Lear. Cornwall has the Earl of Gloucester brought in.

He comes in as a prisoner and Cornwall and Regan cross-question him. He answers their questions with gravity and nobility. One of his loyal servants dies in trying to defend him. This servant, in his struggles, wounds the Duke of Cornwall seriously. The Duke puts out Gloucester's eyes and thrusts him out of gates of his own castle. Two of his servants, however, follow him secretly, with bandages and balm. They decide to send Edgar with him to guide him to Dover. It is a highly ironical situation, for Gloucester does not recognise his own son.

This is a very long Act containing seven scenes. It is also the central Act of the play. It shows the King undergoing terrible sufferings as a result of which his character undergoes a change. But the suffering is too intense for him to bear and it takes away his reason. This Act also shows the undeserved sufferings of Gloucester. He is blinded and driven out of his own house. The heroes of both the main plot and sub-plot have reached the lowest point of their career. In showing Gloucester's blinding on the stage Shakespeare has flouted Aristotle's rules.

Act IV, sc. i

Shakespeare locates this scene on the heath. This is the fourth of such scenes, known as the heath-scenes. In this play the heath is associated with unbearable suffering. It is like hell in that sinners are punished here—or purgatory.

The scene opens with a soliloquy from Edgar in which he expresses his acceptance of misfortunes and as soon as the soliloquy is over the Earl of Gloucester enters, led by an old man. Edgar is deeply moved when he sees the condition of his father who, himself in distress, reflects upon man's miserable state and voices Shakespeare's darkest view:

> As flies to wanton boys are we to the gods;
> They kill us for their sport.[21]

Gloucester tells the old man to bring Edgar some clothes. He then asks Edgar if he knows the way to Dover. He gives Edgar the little money that he has and then they set out for Dover. He tells Edgar to take him to a certain cliff and he will reward

Edgar suitably. Actually he means to kill himself by jumping off the cliff, but this is not made clear here.

Act IV thus begins in a quiet manner. This scene brings the estranged father and son together, though the father does not recognise his son. He is in a highly penitent mood for this treatment of Edgar and the trust he put on Edmund. This scene gives a famous instance of dramatic irony, for Gloucester says:

> Oh! dear son Edgar,
> The food of thy abused father's wrath,
> Might I but live to see thee in my touch,
> I'd say I had eyes again.[22]

He has his wish granted, for Edgar takes his arm to guide him, but his father cannot recognise him. To him Edgar is "the naked fellow", poor Tom the madman. Thus, though he ascribes inhuman cruelty to the gods, it is seen that they are not totally cruel, for he has been united with his son.

Act IV, sc. ii

By this time Goneril and Edmund have come to the palace of the Duke of Albany and the scene takes place in front of the palace. The Duke of Cornwall had sent them (in Act III, sc. vii) to enlist Albany's help and thus this scene becomes linked to the former one.

Oswald, who had come with Goneril and Edmund had gone into the palace to acquaint Albany with all the events that had taken place and had found him in a strange mood. His reactions to the different items of the news were the exact opposites of what Goneril wanted. This makes her realise that Albany has now turned against her and she decides that she herself will adopt a more masterful attitude and disregard her husband altogether. She admires Edmund and makes this clear by giving him a token of her favour and tells him to go back to Cornwall.

After he has gone Albany comes and delivers a diatribe against Goneril, but she pays him no heed. Instead of being frightened or ashamed she abuses him. In the meantime, a messenger comes to inform him that the Duke of Cornwall is

dead. This death is the result of the wound he had received
from Gloucester's servant in the earlier scene (*Vide* the analysis
of Act III, sc., vii *supra*). He is the first evil character to die.

The messenger has brought a letter to Goneril from Regan.
The first thought in Goneril's heart is that she has sent
Edmund to Regan and, since Regan is now a widow, she will
be able to marry Edmund. She is afraid that perhaps Edmund
will succumb to Regan's charms. Albany questions the messenger
more closely and then exclaims:

> Gloucester, I live
> To thank thee for the love thou showd'st the King
> And to revenge thine eyes.[23]

The scene thus establishes firm links with Act III, sc. vii
and also looks forward to the future scenes. It shows several
things. First of all it throws light on the relationship between
Goneril and Edmund. Secondly it shows that Albany is now
entirely against Goneril. Thirdly it gives the news of the Duke
of Cornwall's death and last of all it shows Albany determining
to take an active part in the ensuing events. We also get
foreshadowing of future events in what Goneril is quick to
perceive: Regan's widowhood makes her free to marry Edmund
who will then become the Duke.

Act IV, sc. iii

We come to Dover at last. The Earl of Kent is talking to a
Gentleman near the camp of the French army. He comes to
know that the King of France has suddenly gone back to
France, leaving Cordelia and the army in the hands of the
Marshal of France. We are also told of Cordelia's reactions to
the letter the Gentleman had shown her. This at once links the
scene to the earlier one in which Kent had sent the Gentleman
with his letter and ring to Cordelia (*Vide* the analysis of Act
III, sc. i, *supra*).

Kent tells the Gentleman that Lear has lucid intervals in
his madness. During these times he knows who he is and
recognises others. At these times, however, he is so ashamed
that he refuses to meet Cordelia. He thinks that his injustice is
unforgiveable.

This scene is entirely in poetry and does not take the action forward to any significant extent. It does, however, acquaint us with the fact that Cordelia has received Kent's letter, and also that King Lear is now in Dover. Thus the reader is led to expect that Cordelia and Lear will meet in near future. We are also told that Lear has lucid intervals in his madness, i.e., the spells of lunacy come and go intermittently. This prepares us for the later scene, known as the union-scene. The description of Cordelia's reaction to the news of the ill-treatment meted out to Lear by the two elder sisters clarifies the fact that she harbours no resentments against her father for the injustice he had done to her.

Act IV, sc. iv

We see Cordelia after a very long interval, for she had not been seen after the first scene of the play. She has a doctor with her and sends out a search-party after Lear. She is also given the message that the British army is marching towards them.

This is a very short scene, entirely in poetry and though, like the foregoing one, it does not take the action forward to any significant extent it shows Cordelia's search for Lear and give the news of the advancing British army.

Act IV, sc. v

In this scene we are once more back with Regan whom we had last seen in the seventh scene of the third Act. She is now a widow (*Vide* the analysis of Act IV, sc. ii, *supra*). Here she is talking to Oswald who had come with a letter of Goneril, addressed to Edmund. This at once makes Regan suspicious, for she herself wants to marry him which she knows Goneril cannot do. Edmund is away from the castle and Oswald wants to go in search of him. Regan takes this opportunity to write him a letter on her own. Oswald thus has to choose between Goneril and Regan, for he carries a letter from each to Edmund. It is not clear whom he is going to serve. He himself is undecided.

This scene, a short and unimportant one, is linked to the second scene of this Act, for the letter Oswald brings was given to him in that scene. It is also related to the next scene for in that one he meets Gloucester and Edmund with the letter.

Act IV, sc. vi

This is the famous Dover-scene or the mock-suicide scene. Edgar, guiding his blind father, has reached Dover. Gloucester asks Edgar whether they have reached the high cliff that he'd wanted to reach. Edgar assures him that they have, and gives a graphic description of the cliff and the sea to be seen far below. It has to be noted that he speaks in poetry and the fine language that is proper to him as a nobleman. He is no longer enacting the role of Poor Tom. Gloucester remarks on this fact, that his language has changed, but Edgar denies that there is any change in him.

After the wonderful description given by Edgar, his father is no longer in any doubt that he is really standing on the cliff. He gives Edgar a purse with a few jewels in it and tells him to go away. Edgar bids him farewell and draws a little further and explains in an aside that he has done this to cure his father of despair. He has realised that the Earl wants to commit suicide and he wants not only to preserve Gloucester from this fate but also to restore his faith in God. Committing suicide is an unforgiveable sin and Edgar wants to save his father.

Gloucester, believing himself to be standing alone at the edge of a cliff, utters a short prayer. He asks the gods to bless Edgar and then throws himself down. As is expected, no harm comes to him and Edgar comes forward. Now he has given up the disguise of Poor Tom and presents himself as a peasant. He tells Gloucester that he has been miraculously saved by God:

> Therefore, happy father
> Think that the clearest gods, who make them
> Of men's impossibilities, have preserved the honours.[24]

Gloucester is now reconciled to his fate and as soon as he has expressed this, Lear comes in. The stage direction says, "Enter Lear, fantastically dressed with flowers." This links this part of the scene with the fourth scene of this Act, in which Cordelia had described him as being crowned with wild country flowers and weeds. He is entirely mad and talks

accordingly. Gloucester recognises the voice. He goes forward
to kiss his hand and the pathos of the scene wrings Edgar's
heart.

Even in his madness Lear recognises his loyal servant and
says in a memorable passage:

> I know thee well enough; thy name is Gloucester
> Thou must be patient; we came crying hither.[25]

A few minutes later Cordelia's search-party arrives. Lear
runs off, with the attendants following him. The Gentleman in
charge of the party lingers a few minutes and tells Edgar that a
battle between the French and the British army is imminent.
After he goes away Edgar introduces himself as a peasant to
Gloucester and offers to lead him to a resting-place. Gloucester
agrees.

Before they can do so, however, Oswald comes in. There is
a reward for Gloucester and on seeing him Oswald is elated,
thinking that he will now be able to claim the reward. Edgar,
speaking a peasant-dialect, tries to prevent him laying hands
on his father and knocks him down. Oswald, realising that he
has received a death-blow, enjoins upon Edgar to take the
letter he is carrying to Edmund and then dies. Thus one of
Goneril's accomplices is removed from the scene. The letter is
from her and it is a love-letter. Edgar is shocked at her perfidy
and keeps the letter for future use. By this time the army
drums can be heard and Edgar leads Gloucester to some safe
place. It is to be noted that he addresses Gloucester as "father"
though he has not revealed his identity. In fact he has been
addressing Gloucester as father after the incident of Gloucester's
useless attempt at suicide.

The scene comes to an end here. It is an important scene as
three things happen in it: Gloucester's suicidal attempt, Lear's
capture by Cordelia's search-party and Oswald's death. This is
the second death on the stage, the first being the death of
Gloucester's loyal servant who gave his life trying to save him
(*Vide* the analysis of Act III, sc. vii, *supra*). The Duke of
Cornwall's death had been reported and did not take place on
the stage.

As far as style goes, this scene has a lot of variety. Poetry is spoken by all the characters, but in addition Lear speaks in prose and Edgar speaks in the dialect of a peasant.

The main plot and the sub-plot are briefly brought together in this scene, for King Lear comes in, for however short a time, and so does Oswald.

Act IV, sc. vii

This is the famous scene in which Lear and Cordelia are re-united. Kent has reached the French camp and asks Cordelia not to disclose his identity. Now King Lear, who is still asleep, is brought and music is played to awaken him.

When Lear wakes up he still dazed with sleep and thinks that he is dead and takes Cordelia for an angel:

> Thou art a soul in bliss, but I am bound
> Upon a wheel of fire, that mine own tears
> Do scald like molten lead.[26]

He speaks with great humility—a humility achieved out of unbearable suffering. He thinks he recognises Cordelia though not quite sure about it:

> Do not laugh at me;
> For as I am man, I think this lady
> To be my child Cordelia.[27]

Cordelia, perhaps in tears, assures him that she is, and Lear can hardly believe it. He asks her to forgive him:

> Pray you now, forget and forgive: I am old and foolish.[28]

Thus the scene draws to a close. Everyone except Kent and a Gentleman goes out and the dialogue between them tells us that a bloody battle is going to be fought.

This is the last scene of this Act. All the other scenes of this Act had been slowly building up dramatic suspense, preparing us for the reunion of Lear and Cordelia and so this is the climactic scene of this Act. It is a short scene, consisting of ninety-seven lines only, and is almost entirely in poetry. It is only when Lear and Cordelia, together with the Doctor and the attendants have left the scene that Kent and the Gentleman talk in prose. This is perfectly in keeping with the elevated mood of the re-union scene. It is also a recognition-scene, for at a superficial level Lear recognises Cordelia and at a much subtler level, he not only recognises himself to be a foolish man, but declares it quite openly. According to classical rules, Recognition or *Anagnorisis* is an essential part of tragedy (*Vide* Chapter 9, Plot, *infra*).

Act V, sc. i

This scene moves back from the French to the British camp. Edmund, Regan and others enter and Edmund sends an officer to take orders from the Duke of Albany. In the meanwhile, Regan tries to find out whether Edmund and Goneril have been lovers. Edmund assures her that this is not the case and that he does not love Goneril. He is being very clever in this, for, now that Regan is a widow he can marry her and be the Duke of Cornwall in addition to being the Earl of Gloucester. In contrast, an adulterous relationship with Goneril would be dangerous and useless.

Albany enters and proposes that they should hold a meeting with the old and experienced officers of the army to determine their future course of action. Before they leave the stage, however, Edgar comes in. He is still disguised as a peasant and has brought the love-letter of Goneril to Edmund. This relates the scene to Act IV, sc. vi in which he had killed Oswald and taken the letter from him. He gives the letter to Albany but does not stay to see him read it. Before Albany can read the letter, Edmund brings the news that the French army is in sight and Albany hurries away without reading the letter.

Now there is a soliloquy from Edmund. He cannot decide between Goneril and Regan and decides to wait till the end of the battle. He is certain that their side will win and hopes that Albany and one of the sisters will be killed. He will then have Lear killed and become the King of England. His Machiavellian characteristics thus become emphasised even more.

We realise that he is a typical malcontent, one who has no love for anyone but himself. He proceeds through life with but one thought in his mind—how to achieve greater and greater prosperity for himself. There is utter disregard for others and

he has no softer side to his personality. Both Goneril and
Regan love him, but he has no moral fibre to reciprocate their
love. All his intrigues and plottings are for his own betterment.
He is one of the most cold-blooded villains of Shakespeare.

Act V, sc. ii

This scene is located in between the two warring camps. It
takes place on a field between the two armies. Edgar and his
father enter and Edgar makes the latter stand under a tree
while he goes out to reconnoitre. Then he comes in, bringing
the news that King Lear's army, i.e., the French army has been
defeated and he and Cordelia have been taken prisoners. This
produces a mood of despair in Gloucester and here Edgar
speaks some of the noblest lines in Shakespeare:

> Men must endure
> Their going hence, even as their coming hither:
> Ripeness is all.[29]

This is the shortest scene in the play, comprising only
eleven lines. This is a scene in which a battle takes place, but it
is the result of the battle that is important and not the battle
itself:

> The shortness of this scene may be rather explained as an
> example of dramatic economy since the battle itself is not
> important. We are only interested in the result of the
> battle.[30]

The noble stoicism of Edgar, exemplified in the lines
quoted above, makes the scene a memorable one. It also looks
forward to the next scene.

Act V, sc. iii

This is the last scene of the play. Many of Shakespeare's
plays have only one long scene in the last Act, as in *The
Merchant of Venice* and *Twelfth Night*. Here, however, there
are three.

The British army has won the battle. Edmund is conquering
hero. He has taken King Lear and Cordelia prisoners. Even in
adversity Cordelia's first thoughts are for her father. On her
own she is ready to face all misfortunes but she is worried for

the King. Lear himself, however, is not worried. He does not mind being in prison, for Cordelia will be with him:

> We two alone will sing like birds i'th'cage:
> When thou dost ask me blessings, I'll kneel down
> And ask of thee forgiveness.[31]

They are led away and Edmund asks for one of the officers. He gives the officer a paper containing the order for the execution of both Lear and Cordelia. He tells the Captain to do this at once but keeps the whole affair a secret from Albany. When Albany and the two sisters come on the stage the former praises him for his part in the war and means to honour him. Before he can do anything the two sisters start quarrelling over Edmund. Albany is forestalled by Regan, because she publicly acknowledges Edmund as her husband. Albany then accuses him and Goneril of high treason and challenges him to prove his innocence by duelling with him. According to the code of chivalry he can be represented by a champion. The challenge is then proclaimed in due form by a herald and Edgar appears in answer to it. He and Edmund fight and Edmund is defeated.

It becomes clear that Albany has read Goneril's letter to Edmund and he confronts her with it. Instead of being ashamed of herself or alarmed, she challenges his right to judge her and leaves the stage. Meanwhile Edmund, realising that he has received his death-blow, undergoes a change of heart. Edgar reveals his identity and speaks some of the most famous lines in Shakespeare, vindicating the justice meted out by the gods:

> The Gods are just, and of our pleasant vices
> Make instruments to plague us;
> The dark and vicious place where thee he got
> Cost him his eyes.[32]

Albany asks him what had befallen him and his father and Edgar tells him everything. Finally he tells him how he had revealed himself to Gloucester and how, after blessing him, Gloucester had passed away.

While they are talking a Gentleman enters carrying a bloody knife and tells everyone that Goneril, after poisoning Regan, has killed herself. Their bodies are brought in. Thus there are two more deaths.

Now Edmund, who has undergone a change of heart, desires to do some good before he dies. He tells them about his order to kill Lear and Cordelia and asks them to send someone to revoke it. But it is already too late and Lear enters with the dead body of Cordelia in his arms. This is the most moving scene in the play and indeed, in the whole of Shakespeare. Dr. Johnson's comments on it have become famous. He was so shocked by Cordelia's death that he could not bear to read the scene for many years. It is generally thought that her death violates the rule of Poetic Justice.

Lear, looking upon the dead body of Cordelia, speaks some of the most moving lines in Shakespeare. His last moments however, are blissful, for he thinks that Cordelia is alive, and then he too dies.

News is brought in that Edmund too is dead. Now that all the royal characters except Albany are dead, the crown of England becomes his by right. He is a truly good and noble person and he offers the crown to Kent and Edgar Kent is too heart-broken at Lear's death and he says he will follow Lear, like a loyal servant, to the other world as he had done in this one. The honour of delivering the epilogue falls on Edgar:

> The oldest hath borne most: we that are young
> Shall never see so much, nor live so long.[33]

The play ends with an overwhelming evocation of the emotion of pity and terror that, according to Aristotle, are the emotions proper to tragedy.

REFERENCES

1. Act I, sc.i, line 61, p. 7.
2. Act I, sc.i, ll. 86-92, p. 9.
3. Act I, sc.i, ll. 104-6, p. 10.
4. Act I, sc.i, ll. 253-56, p. 19.
5. Nicoll, Allardyce, *Studies in Shakespeare*, London, 1927, pp. 154-55.

6. Act I, sc.ii, ll. 180-81, p. 32.

7. Act I, sc.iii, ll. 17-19, p. 33.

8. Empson, W., *The Structure of Complex Words*, p. 129.

9. Act I, sc. iv, ll. 100-101, p. 39.

10. Act I, sc. iv, ll. 145-47, p. 41.

11. Act I, sc. iv, ll. 285-87, p. 49.

12. Act I, sc. v, ll. 43-44, p. 55.

13. Act III, sc. ii, ll. 16-18, p. 101.

14. Act III, sc. ii, ll. 59-60, p. 103.

15. Act III, sc. ii, ll. 68-69, p. 104.

16. Act III, sc. iv, ll. 12-14, p. 107.

17. Act III, sc. iv, ll. 29-36, p. 108.

18. Act III, sc. iv, ll. 48-49, p. 109.

19. Empson, W., *op. cit.*, p. 137.

20. Act III, sc. v, ll. 19-20, p. 121.

21. Act IV, sc. i, ll. 36-37, p. 140.

22. Act IV, sc. i, ll. 21-24, p. 139.

23. Act IV, sc. ii, ll. 94-96, p. 150.

24. Act IV, sc. vi, ll. 72-74, p. 162.

25. Act IV, sc. vi, ll. 175-76, p. 169.

26. Act IV, sc. vii, ll. 46-48, p. 178.

27. Act IV, sc. vii, ll. 68-70, p. 179.

28. Act IV, sc. vii, ll. 84, p. 180.

29. Act V, sc. ii, ll. 9-11, p. 186.

30. Muir, K., *op. cit.*, p. 185.

31. Act V, sc. iii, ll. 9-11, p. 187.

32. Act V, sc. iii,. ll. 169-71, p. 197.

33. Act V, sc. iii, ll. 324-5, p. 206.

6

The Major Themes

The central theme of any work is the main idea that holds the work together. It may so happen that the construction of a play might meander, and be haphazard and flabby, for the writer may not be a good craftsman, but the message he wants to convey (i.e. the central theme) is so strongly and convincingly expressed that the play gives the impression of being a neatly unified whole. The theme, thus, is an extremely important part of any work. It is not necessary for a work to have only one theme. It might have a major theme, side by side with many sub-themes. Shakespeare's plays are so complex that most of the time there are many themes in one play. Moreover, a complex work can be interpreted from many points of view and different critics have posited different themes for his plays. *King Lear* is one of those plays that have been studied from many viewpoints, some of which are given below.

(a) The Theme of Redemption

A.C. Bradley has put so much stress on this theme that he said that the play can be named *The Redemption of King Lear*. According to this view we see King Lear, an obstinate, arrogant and rather foolish old man, being gradually purged of the imperfections in his nature and led to a nobility that is the true nobility of the spirit, far higher than mere nobility of birth or social position:

> The business of "the Gods" with him was neither to torment him, nor to teach him a "noble anger", but to lead him to attain through apparently hopeless failure the very end and aim of life.[1]

In the beginning of the play we see Lear in the full glory of his royalty, the powerful and benevolent giver of largesse. The only thing he insists on is that his daughters publicly admit their love for him. In spite of his old age he retains and reveals immaturity in this matter. The division of the kingdom thus becomes just an unnecessary farce because the division had already been made before the love-test. When Cordelia, his favourite daughter, instead of supporting him in this game, proves to be a spoil-sport he becomes inordinately angry. This is but the proof of hurt pride and also of childish immaturity. When the Earl of Kent interposes he banishes him, which is the action of a man who cannot bear any kind of opposition. Then, most foolishly, he gives away all his powers and becomes totally dependent on Goneril and Regan, never thinking of the possible consequences.

The blows of an unkind Fate then commence to shower on him and gradually he realises how very foolish and unjust he has been. When Goneril and Regan ill-treat him he is justifiably angry and curses them, but as yet he is thinking only of himself. Then on the heath, even before he has seen Poor Tom and learnt how low a man might be brought in the world, he is already praying for the poor. He blames himself for not having paid attention to the condition of his poor subjects. True humility, however, has not come yet. It comes only after he has recovered from madness. Then, indeed, he looks upon himself as a foolish old man and even confesses that he may not be fully in his senses. Now at last he achieves true humility and maturity of character. This maturity is expressed the best when he says:

> Upon such sacrifices, my Cordelia,
> The Gods themselves throw incense.[2]

This gradual progress of Lear, according to Bradley, is the central theme of the play, and many are the critics who agree with him. Coleridge, for example, pronounces that Lear's character is the main concern:

> ...the mind and mood of the person whose character, passions and sufferings are the main *subject-matter* of the play.[3]

One feels the justice of this view, and more or less the same view, with slight modifications, is found in later critics as well. C.J. Sisson for example says:

> We have long ago learnt to recognise in its action and development a theme which might justify the title *The Redemption of King Lear*.[4]

This critic traces the development of Lear's character in the play and compares it with some other plays of Shakespeare, affirming that it is a theme that recurs many times in his works. Furthermore, taking Greek tragedy, Milton and Shelley as examples, he says that this is a theme that goes beyond Shakespearean drama, for it is a religious theme concerning the soul:

> ...the reconciliation in *King Lear* comes despite the evil in the world...in the fulfillment of a soul's destiny.[5]

(b) The Theme of Incongruity

G. Wilson Knight explains that *King Lear* presents a mass of incongruities that cannot be reconciled with each other and that this is the basic idea of the play. In other tragedies also the incongruities of life are presented and reconciled in the evocation of masterly passions and in comedies they are reconciled in laughter and humour. *King Lear* stands out as a special case, for in it the incongruities that are presented are not resolved:

> In *King Lear* there is a dualism continually crying out in vain to be resolved either by tragedy or by comedy.[6]

The most important incongruity in the play is to be found in the character of the King himself. He has great capacities for love in his heart, so great that the destruction of this love by his daughters destroys his mind itself—he becomes mad:

> A tremendous soul is, as it were, incongruously geared to a puerile intellect.[7]

This intellect is so poor that as soon as he realises the falsity of his daughters, it snaps. Knight calls it "the love-theme" and relates it to "the Gloucester-theme". Gloucester himself, in his speech about eclipses, mentions these incongruities early in the play:

> ...love cools, friendship falls off, brothers divide...there is son against father: the King falls from bias of nature; there is father against child.[8]

It is a long speech, giving instances of many such incongruities and Wilson Knight says:

> Gloucester's words hint a universal incongruity here: the fantastic incongruity of parent and child opposition.[9]

The play then proceeds to give a series of incongruities: Lear is childlike in mind, but titanic in passion, Goneril and Regan profess an exaggeratedly intense love for him but behave with unnatural cruelty. Cordelia professes to love him according to her duty and hides her true and intense love for him. Kent intercedes to plead for sanity and justice but he is banished for his loyalty. The entire play is a catalogue of such incongruities.

It is on the basis of such incongruities that Wilson Knight argues that there is a grotesque and macabre humour in the play. Thus, as incongruity is the central theme of the play and all these incongruities are as grotesquely comic as tragic, he comes to the logical conclusion that the play is a paradoxical one in that it defeats it own tragic purpose:

> *King Lear* is supreme in that in this main theme it faces the very absence of tragic purpose.... The tragic purification of the essentially untragic is yet complete.[10]

(c) Man and the Universe

It has also been asserted that in this play Shakespeare has explored the intricate relationship of man with the universe. This has been one of the views expressed by G. Wilson Knight. In the preceding section we have seen how he stresses the element of incongruity in the play, taking that to be the main theme. At the same time he tells us:

> Mankind's relation to the universe is its theme and Edgar's trumpet is as the universal judgement summoning vicious men to account.[11]

The fact that the same critic could say that the play is centred around different themes shows the richness and complexity of the work. This is proof enough that interpretation of Shakespeare's works is inexhaustible. There can never be any opinion on them that can be taken as the last word on any of them.

It is perfectly true that the plight of King Lear and his experiences cannot be taken as befalling just any ordinary individual. King Lear, according to G. Wilson Knight, is not just a man but mankind itself. His awful sufferings are the sufferings to be undergone by mankind before he can be ready for salvation. The play, as Wilson Knight says, presents the travails of only six characters: Lear, Kent, Gloucester, Edmund, Edgar and Cordelia. Yet through them a whole universe and a whole race are represented. These characters, however great and distinctly individualised, are not mere individuals, or the figments of a poet's imagination. Their associations and implications reach out to encompass the entire mankind:

> *King Lear* is a tragic vision of humanity, in its complexity, its interplay of purpose, its travailing evolution. The play is a microcosm of the human race.[12]

(d) The Theme of Renunciation

It has been pointed out that right at the beginning of the play King Lear renounces his throne and with it his powers. Throughout the play this theme is reinforced again and again. It has, therefore, been argued by George Orwell that the central theme of the play is that of renunciation:

> The subject of Lear is renunciation, and it is only by being wilfully blind that one can fail to understand what Shakespeare is saying.[13]

When we look at the story of the play from this point of view, it can be seen that this is a very valid theme. The note of renunciation is struck right in the beginning of the play. Lear announces that he is going to withdraw from all the complexities of ruling a kingdom and is going to divide the land among his daughters. After this has been done, he further announces that he will keep nothing but the title of the King and a hundred knights for the retinue fitting for a king. Addressing Goneril, Regan and their husbands he says:

> I do invest you jointly with my powers,
> Pre-eminence, and all the large effects
> That troop with majesty ... ...
> ... ... Only, we shall retain
> The name and all the addition to a king; the sway
> Revenue, execution of the rest,
> Beloved sons, be yours.[14]

The rest of the play only dramatises the result of this extremely foolish renunciation. The play thus, as Orwell opines, explores the effect and the possibilities of this initial act of renunciation. Lear himself never forgets it and does not allow the audience to forget, either. There are numerous references to this throughout the play. Either he, or the Fool, is constantly referring to it. Instead of bringing happiness and tranquillity, Lear's renunciation brings only suffering and conflict.

(e) Parent-Child Relationship

Along with the others, this is taken to be one of the themes of the play. Kenneth Muir, while not making clear what, according to him, the main theme is, yet points out that this is one of the themes:

> One theme of the play, expressed in plot and under-plot, is the parent-child relationship.[15]

This, indeed, is very clearly to be seen in the play. The main plot presents the relationship between parent and child in two different ways. Thus there is King Lear's relationship with Goneril and Regan. This is based at first on deception and the nature of the deception is clear to all but the father himself. The dialogue between the two sisters at the end of the scene shows how freely they criticise him:

Regan: 'Tis the infirmity of his age; yet he hath ever but slenderly known himself.

Goneril: The best and soundest of his time hath been but rash; then must we look from his age to receive

alone the imperfection of long-engraffed
condition, but therewithal the unruly waywardness
that infirm and choleric years bring with them.[16]

In other words, these two sisters have no love or tenderness
for their father. Instead they have contempt. This is their side
of the question. Lear himself makes it quite clear that he loves
Cordelia more than the two of them. This argues a lukewarm
love for his elder daughters. Though he divides Cordelia's
portion of the kingdom between them, he does it out of pique.
So this relationship is based on a foundation of sand and
crumbles at the first touch. Goneril and Regan betray and
insult him at the first opportunity and Lear, the minute he
realises Goneril's hypocrisy, breaks out in the most terrible
curse that can be uttered against a woman—that of barrenness.

His relationship with Cordelia is definitely a most positive
relationship but it is eclipsed at first by his anger and obstinacy.
Cordelia, disgusted by his demands of public avowal of her
natural love for him as well as by the hypocrisy of her sisters
refuses to gratify him. Lear, out of disappointment, disinherits
her. It is only at the end that the wonderful quality of their
genuine love finally reveals itself. Indeed, it is difficult to find
a parallel to the re-union scene. Lear is still dazed and Cordelia
is so choked by tears that she can hardly speak:

Lear: If you have poison for me, I will drink it.
           I know you do not love me; for your sisters
           Have, as I do remember, done me wrong:
           You have some cause, they have not.
Cordelia: No cause, no cause.[17]

This is true paternal and filial love—ready to sacrifice itself for
the other, forgiving and forgetting all wrongs, finding a prison
to be paradise:

Come, let's away to prison;
We two alone will sing like birds i'th' cage.[18]

In no other play of Shakespeare has the parent-child relationship
been so movingly explored. It is not at all surprising that Lear
should die when Cordelia is killed.

The sub-plot also echoes the same theme. Here also there is a father with two sons, one of whom gives him true filial love and the other does everything he can to destroy him. Here again we see how parental love is misled at first, for Gloucester lavishes his love on the malcontent of the play. He believes in Edmund's allegations against Edgar and, without even talking to Edgar, lets Edmund drive him out. Then comes retribution in the shape of his own betrayal by Edmund. He is made to suffer as much as Lear is. He is not allowed to commit suicide and Edgar does not reveal his identity to him till the very last moment. It is already too late by that time and he does not stay alive to enjoy the bliss:

> His flawed heart,
> Alack, too weak the conflict to support
> Twixt two extremes of passion, joy and grief,
> Burst smilingly.[19]

We see how Shakespeare explores the theme of parent-child relationship from many different points of view. One relevant point in this respect is that both in the main and the sub-plot he has taken up the relationship between father and child, not of mother and child. He has, however, presented two different relationships (father and daughter, and father and son) and presented them in four different ways (the positive and the negative way).

(f) The Theme of Disruption

This theme can be understood when the play is placed against the theories related to Elizabethan view of the universe. They believed in the Great Chain of Being, in which every living creature had its own place, with God at the summit. The same scheme is reflected in human society where the King represents God and is at the top of the social scale. All human beings, in several stages, come below the King. This social and cosmological order had to be preserved, for a disruption of this order will bring about chaos. The theory is actually much more complex, and includes ethical and moral orders as well. In *King Lear* we see a disruption of this social and moral order. Lear, for example, divides his kingdom in an unjust manner, thus challenging the ethical rules. His violation of ethical rules rebound upon him when Goneril and Regan act in an unnatural manner. They violate, not only the supreme authority of the King but also the supreme authority of the father in the family, thus bringing about disorder and chaos in society.

This disorder is reflected in the sub-plot as well. Edmund turns against his father and his brother and destroys the family. Moreover, both Goneril and Regan are attracted to him and he means to take advantage of this in such a manner as to get the throne of England, to which he has no right. Goneril turns against her husband, thus violating sacred religious and family ties, and then poisons her own sister. In every way, the play stresses unnatural violation of religious, social and familial rules:

> Disruption in the kingdom, disruption in the family...were facets of that universal disruption of Nature...which for millennia had been a standard of mankind.... *King Lear* is an exploration of this potential.[20]

(g) Contrast between Two Aspects

King Lear is a play in which it is almost impossible to consider the theme separately from the character of the hero. The two merge into each other. Frank Kermode equalises the two and finds that the King embodies the theme:

> In this play, not for the first time, Shakespeare concerns himself with the contrast between the two bodies of the king: one lives by ceremony...distinguished by the regalia which set him above nature. The other is born naked, subject to disease and pain.[21]

We find the first aspect in the first scene. Lear is indeed all-powerful in it. He can, and does, divide a whole country arbitrarily into different portions and distributes them as so many pieces of cake. He can also banish from his kingdom whoever incurs his wrath, like the Duke of Kent.

But then, this is the first and the last time we see him playing God with hundreds of men and women, reigning over them with Divine Right. Then there is a rapid fall from this state of worldly power and glory. It comes by different stages and it takes the King some time to realise this gradual degradation. His Fool is beaten up, his messenger the disguised Duke of Kent is put in the stocks, his knights are dismissed and finally he is out on the heath on a stormy night.

So Lear is stripped and moves from the ceremonies of the first scene to the company of a naked "nature", the thing itself.[22]

Thus Lear is brought to the same level that Poor Tom has reached, and finally he is shorn even of reason. Nothing remains but the naked self—man as he is born a 'forked animal'. The play presents the contrast between the former artificial self and the later natural self.

These are only a few of the themes that literary critics have found in *King Lear*. Many other themes and sub-themes have been found in the play. As a matter of fact, *King Lear* is such a complex play that it will continue to be interpreted in different ways by different critics in the ages to come.

REFERENCES

1. Bradley, A.C., *Shakespearean Tragedy*. London: Macmillan and Co., 1960, p. 235.

2. Act V, sc. iii, ll. 20-21, p. 188.

3. Kermode, F., ed., *Shakespeare: King Lear: A Casebook*. London: Macmillan, 1978, p. 34.

4. Sisson, C.J., *Justice in King Lear*, in Kermode, F., *op. cit.*, p. 235.

5. *Ibid.*, p. 243.

6. Knight, G. W., *King Lear and the Comedy of the Grotesque*, in Kermode, *op. cit.*, p. 119.

7. *Ibid.*, p. 120.

8. Act I, sc. ii, ll. 100-114, pp. 28-29.

9. Knight, G.W., *op. cit.*, p. 121.

10. *Ibid.*, p. 134.

11. Bratchell, D.F., ed., *Shakespearean Tragedy*. London: Routledge, 1990, p. 132.

12. *Ibid.*

13. Orwell, G., *Lear, Tolstoy and the Fool*, in Kermode, *op. cit.*, p. 160.

14. Act I, sc. i, ll. 129-137, pp. 11-12.

15. Muir, K., *op. cit.*, p. xlvii.
16. Act I, sc. i, ll. 292-98, pp. 21-22.
17. Act IV, sc. vii, ll. 72-75, p. 179.
18. Act V, sc. iii, ll. 8-9, p. 187.
19. Act V, sc. iii, ll. 195-98, p. 198.
20. Holloway, J., *King Lear*, in Kermode *op. cit.*, p. 207.
21. Kermode, F., *op. cit.*, p. 20.
22. *Ibid.*

7

The Major Characters

(a) Shakespeare's Characters

A play, in order to pass triumphantly the test of time, must have strong as well as lifelike characters, and our poet stands unrivalled in this sphere. His characters are more than realistic and three-dimensional beings, for they often get a symbolic dimension, thus becoming universal figures. Some dramatists depict their central figures with aplomb but their other characters remain vague and shadowy, as is the case with Marlowe. Shakespeare on the other hand (save for the early plays) depicts all characters with so much individualisation that they gain a personality that is peculiar to them.

It has also to be remembered that it is he who has given more memorable dramatic characters than any other dramatist. His tragic heroes, like King Lear and others, his heroines, like Rosalind among numerous others have become immortal. Other dramatists have given one or two such figures but Shakespeare has given an entire portrait-gallery.

Moreover, he never reached a point of stasis in his art of characterisation, or, indeed, in any other field of his art. As he himself grew older in life his understanding of his fellow human beings also developed and consequently his delineations became fuller and grew in range and variety. All the depths of the human mind were plumbed and all the complexities explored. What Pope had said two centuries ago is still valid:

His characters are so much Nature herself that 'tis a sort of injury to call them by so distant a name as copies of her.[1]

This expertise was acquired slowly, but surely and painstakingly. The first phase of his career shows him learning his art and so there are evidences of immaturity. The characters of the second phase already show more understanding of human nature. The important male figures of the Chronicle plays are the creation of this time as well as the memorable heroines of the golden comedies. The four heroines of these comedies cast their male counterparts into shade, so captivating are they.

The great tragic heroes belong to the third phase. Here a world is presented in which evil predominates. Hamlet, Othello, Lear and Macbeth were created at this time. Such characters are not merely realistic, for they have attained the status of universality, and therefore represent the 'character universal'.

Shakespeare went on to create more memorable characters, male as well as female, in his last Romances, but the titanic figure of the tragic hero does not recur any longer. The present work is concerned more intimately with such a figure and his associates, though Cordelia, in her innocence and purity, foreshadows the later heroines.

In creating his characters Shakespeare had not only real life, but many other supporting elements, to fall back upon. Contemporary customs and stage-rules were there to provide a base, as well as classical precepts and examples. Rules for characterisation had been explicitly formulated by Aristotle and practical examples were to be found in classical drama. It has been already pointed out (*Vide* Chapter 3, *Life and Works, supra*), Shakespeare had studied Plautus and Terence in comedy and Seneca in tragedy, during his schooldays. Many other contemporary works on the subject were also available, like Thomas Newton's *The Touchstone of Complexions*, Hall's *Characters of Virtues and Vices*, Overbury's *Characters*, etc. These, in addition to rules, contained sketches of characters to which a dramatist could turn. Theophrastus (whose work was translated by Boyes) had given more than a hundred of such characters.

The tradition of giving character-sketches had been started

by Aristotle who had given six such in his *Ethics*. He had laid down the rules governing dramatic characters in his *Poetics*. All characters, whether tragic or comic, should have four traits: (a) Proportion or Goodness, (b) Appropriateness, (c) Realism, and (d) Consistency.

The quality of Proportion or Goodness has two implications. The moral intention of a character must be good:

> Any speech or action that manifests moral purpose of any kind will be expressive of character: the character will be good if the purpose is good.[2]

Aristotle points out that this goodness differs from person to person as is perfectly natural. Goodness, moreover, must not be un-adulterated in a character for that would not be lifelike. Goodness and evil must exist in proper proportion in a character, just as it does in real life.

Appropriateness or Propriety is the second quality. A character should act or speak in accordance with the kind of person he is:

> There is a type of manly valour; but valour in a woman, or unscrupulous cleverness, is inappropriate.[3]

There is no violation of this rule in our poet. The characters always speak and act in such a manner as is appropriate of their age and social position. This is so faithfully done that when a character adopts a disguise he speaks in accordance with the persona he adopts. Edgar, the Earl's son is totally different from Edgar as Poor Tom.

The third quality specified by Aristotle is Realism. He points out that this quality is different from the first two, but he does not expatiate upon it. Shakespeare's characters are always true to life. Their actions and speeches, given the situation, are always natural and realistic. When Cordelia refuses to flatter her foolish father in the love-test, it is perfectly natural. Likewise, what can be more true to life than her loving care for him in the re-union scene?

The fourth quality, Consistency, is the most important of all for this means that the character must remain true to his own nature. King Lear is presented as an impulsive, hot-headed man. He remains so till his very reason goes. Thereafter, there is change, but it is not surprising that such traumatic experiences should bring about a change in his character. Aristotle has pointed out that a character can change if such change can be credibly brought about by the circumstances, and also that the character must remain recognizably the same. Both of these conditions have been fulfilled.

The delineation of characters in Elizabethan drama thus depended on two factors. On one hand there are the classical rules and on the other the practical sketches given by the ancient and the contemporary writers. Shakespeare and the other writers of the time had easy access to all these. Yet it is Shakespeare who has given us so many memorable characters. What is even more admirable is that he accepted the conventions and, when necessary, also adapted them to suit his needs. Henri Fluchère has stressed this aspect of his art:

> It is equally undeniable that, allowing for his own peculiar genius, he conforms with the accepted conventions of character-drawing as with other conventions.[4]

In addition to all these features there is the towering figure of the tragic hero about whom there are many specific rules laid down by Aristotle and his commentators. Besides these theories, Shakespeare had the practical example of other tragic heroes in Latin and English plays, particularly those of Seneca, Marlowe and Kyd. The most important rules laid down by Aristotle concerning the tragic hero, in addition to the four features mentioned above, are that he must be better than the average, of noble birth and nature, and that he must have some kind of flaw in his nature. Of these, it is the third aspect that is the most important. This has come to be known as "the tragic flaw" which brings inevitable tragic doom. Aristotle says:

> A man who is not eminently good and just, yet whose misfortune is brought about not by vice or depravity but by some error or frailty.[5]

This is "hamartia", which essentially means an error of

judgement that leads the tragic hero to commit a mistake that brings about his tragic downfall. This error of judgement, in Elizabethan times, came to encompass a serious shortcoming in the character, like indecision in Hamlet, jealousy in Othello, ambition in Macbeth etc. It need not, however, mean any such destructive trait. An imperfection that leads a man to commit a crime imperils the nobility of the character, but an error of judgement does not turn him into a criminal. Thus, while Macbeth goes on piling crime upon crime he loses our sympathy and respect, which the ideal tragic hero should not. Aristotle is careful to point out that the flaw in the character is not a serious one, but merely an error or a frailty in a man who is otherwise worthy of respect. He clearly says that in tragedy the hero must be better than the average man and thus inspire respect:

> Tragedy is an imitation of persons who are above the common level.... The poet, in representing men who are irascible or indolent, or have such other defects of character, should present the type and yet ennoble it.[6]

As we shall see, the character of King Lear is truly that of an ideal tragic hero from the Aristotelian view.

(b) King Lear

Lear is one of those characters who offer inexhaustible scope for interpretations. If the student makes a selection of only a few of the critical opinions on him he will be bewildered at and overwhelmed with their variety. Let us first consider him as a tragic hero, and then we shall consider other views.

He is the ideal classical tragic hero. To take the most obvious point first, he is noble by birth as well as by nature. Aristotle had said:

> He must be one who is highly renowned and prosperous— a personage like Oedipus, Theyestes or other illustrious men of such families.[7]

King Lear, the King of Britain, is definitely a "highly renowned and prosperous" personage, with a noble heritage. Aristotle also says that we have persons who are "above the common level" and this too is true of him. He is definitely of a stature above that of the common man. There are critics who have equated him with Christ (*Vide* Chapter 6, *Themes*, *supra*). This would not have been possible if he had been below, or even like, the average man. All these however, are not so important as the feature of *hamartia*—that flaw in the character which brings about the tragic doom.

When we take up this aspect of Lear we see that herein is he the most ideal tragic hero among the four great tragic heroes of Shakespeare. Aristotle makes it quite clear that he considers the tragic hero to be a man not exceptionally good, but one with enough human frailty to make mistakes. The tragic hero has to arouse pity and terror:

> ...pity is aroused by unmerited misfortune, fear by the misfortunes of a man like ourselves.[8]

Now King Lear, though a king and nobler than the average man, is yet a man, not a divine or semi-divine being as in many Greek tragedies, nor a sub-human creature. He has the basic requirements of an Aristotelian hero—good but not too good; ordinary enough to make a mistake, yet worthy of our respect. The flaw in him that leads him to make the error of judgement, his *hamartia*, is most significantly the same as that of the ideal Greek tragic hero, Oedipus. It is *hybris* or overweening self-confidence and arrogance. This is so much a part of Lear's nature that he is not even aware of it. Coleridge has pointed out this trait. He has always been regarded as God's representative on earth, every whim of his has been satisfied, he does not know what it is to be disappointed and he takes it for granted that whatever he does is right. This has given rise to *hybris*, which is always punished by the gods in Greek tragedies:

> A long life of absolute power, in which he has been flattered to the top of his bent, has produced in him that blindness to human limitations and that presumptuous self-will which in Greek tragedies we have so often seen stumbling against the alter of Nemesis.[9]

It is this that makes him fly into a rage when Cordelia refuses to satisfy his childish whim. Outraged by the statement of Cordelia he makes his fatal error of judgement of disowning her and divesting himself of all powers in favour of the two elder daughters. His *hamartia* does not lead him to commit terrible crimes like murder and such, as the other Shakespearean heroes do. It really and truly is only an error of judgement.

It has been pointed out that Lear commits not one, but three errors. He does not understand the true nature of kingship. It is true that the King has divine rights, but along with the rights go the responsibilities of kingship. A King must rule wisely over his subjects and Lear is anything but wise. He has, as he himself admits later, never given a thought to those of his subjects who are poor and destitute. In the first scene he banishes Kent merely out of pique and reveals himself as an irresponsible ruler. He does not understand the nature of love. True love like Cordelia's does not advertise itself. Nor does he understand the implications of the language in which his daughters couch their love. The language used by the two elder daughters is hyperbolical and artificial whereas Cordelia makes use of deliberate understatement. Lear shows himself as totally without understanding:

> Lear then invites tragedy by three errors of judgement—error with regard to the nature of kingship, the nature of love and the nature of language.[10]

But this is not all. No one theory can explain the grandeur and complexity of Lear's nature. He is a much more complex figure than Sophocles's King Oedipus, for Shakespeare allows him to attain spiritual salvation by making him recognise the imperfections in himself, by making him repent and become humble. When he sees Poor Tom he becomes aware of his ignorance and neglect of his poor subjects and cries out:

> O! I have ta'en
> Too little care of this. Take physic, pomp;
> Expose thyself to feel what wretches feel,
> That thou mayst shake the superflux to them,
> And show the Heavens more just.[11]

This is how he takes the first step towards spiritual upliftment—by sympathising with the poor. After this comes his madness—

the lowest point reached by him. Then with the restoration of
his reason there is a total change in him. The arrogant, foolish,
obstinate old man has now recognised his own frailties and
become humble:

> Pray do not mock me:
> I am a very foolish fond old man,
> Fourscore and upwards, not an hour more or less;
> And, to deal plainly,
> I fear I am not in my perfect mind.[12]

This is not enough, for he goes further, asking Cordelia to
forgive him. After saying that Cordelia has every right not to
love him he says that if she gives him poison he will gladly
drink it, he says:

> Pray you now, forget and forgive; I am old and foolish.[13]

He is now pure of heart, and shall see God, as Christ had
promised. Herein he has gone far beyond the limits of the
classical tragic hero, yet, from that point of view one feature
still remains to be noted. Aristotle has given *Anagnorisis*
(Recognition) as one of the features of plot, but it is no less
relevant for characters. Lear's recognition of himself as a
foolish old man is the best and most subtle kind of *anagnorisis*
that a dramatist can give.

Interpreting Lear as a classical tragic hero is but only one
way of understanding him. There are scores of interpretations,
a few of which are given below:

A.W. Schlegel:	Lear is choleric, overbearing and almost childish from age.... But he has a warm and affectionate heart.
Coleridge:	He is the open and ample play-room of Nature's passions.
Lamb:	The greatness of Lear is not in corporal dimensions, but in intellectual.
Harley Granville-Barker	More a magnificent portent than a man.
G. Wilson Knight:	A tremendous soul is, as it were, geared to a puerile intellect.[14]

(c) Earl of Gloucester

The Earl of Gloucester is the chief character of the sub-plot, and is, in many ways, a minor counterpart of Lear. This feature had been noticed by the early critics like Schlegel and it has been repeatedly emphasised in the last century:

The Gloster-theme throughout reflects and emphasises and exaggerates all the pre-current qualities of the Lear-theme.[15]

Gloucester is the tragic hero of the sub-plot just as Lear is that of the main one. As such, like Lear, he fulfils the Aristotelian requirements. He is nobly born and is also noble by nature. His *hamartia*, just like Lear's, is to be mistaken in his offspring. He lavished care and affection on the undeserving Edmund. It is noticeable that in the first scene it is Edmund whom he takes to Court and recommends him to the Earl of Kent.

When he sees Edmund seemingly hiding a letter and makes him give it to him he is instantly convinced of Edgar's villainy. He does not even realise that the handwriting is that of Edmund and not of Edgar.

After this Edmund manages things in such a way that he does not meet Edgar at all. As a matter of fact, he does not meet Edgar in the entire play. When he does meet Edgar after his blinding, the latter is in disguise. He believes in whatever Edmund says.

Gloucester's error of judgement, thus, like Lear's brings tragic doom upon him. He is a loyal subject of the King and tries to help him and this brings misfortune upon him—his eyes are put out and he is driven out of his own castle.

It is when he is blind that the realisation of Edmund's villainy comes upon him and he acknowledges his own folly openly:

> I stumbled when I saw. Full oft 'tis seen,
> Our means secure us, and our mere defects
> Prove our commodities. Oh! dear son Edgar,
> The food of thy abused father's wrath,
> Might I but live to see thee in my touch,
> I'd say I had eyes again.[16]

God grants his prayer and he does meet his dear son, but Shakespeare here introduces an improbability or incongruity (as different critics have repeatedly pointed out) by making him unable to recognise Edgar by his voice. Not only here, but later when, after he has failed to commit suicide, Edgar meets him again as a peasant (not as Poor Tom) he fails to recognise Edgar's voice, either as that of Poor Tom or as that of his own son. Yet, when King Lear enters as fully mad, he recognises his voice.

His inability to recognise the handwriting in the incriminating letter and his inability to recognise his son's voice are two of the improbabilities of the play. Apart from these, however, Gloucester's career proceeds like that of a tragic hero. His self-recognition, like that of Lear's is the best kind of *anagnorisis*, for, as Aristotle requires, it arises out of the circumstances quite naturally and is therefore fully credible.

Shakespeare has portrayed him as a rather credulous person who believes in superstitions:

> These late eclipses in the sun and
> Moon portend no good to us.[17]

It is to be expected that such persons would have faith in religion yet after his misfortunes he loses all faith in God. Shakespeare gives him the most pessimistic lines that he has ever written:

> As flies to wanton boys are we to th'Gods;
> They kill us for their sport.[18]

Edgar saves him from committing the unforgiveable sin of suicide and Gloucester's attitude changes from one of despair to one of acceptance:

> ...henceforth I'll bear
> Affliction till it do cry out itself
> "Enough, enough."[19]

Shakespeare gives him a pleasant death, for when at last Edgar reveals his identity, he dies a blissful death:

> His flawed heart,
> Alas, too weak the conflict to support!

'Twixt two extremes of passion, joy and grief,
Burst smilingly.[20]

Gloucester has been looked upon mainly as a lesser
counterpart of or a complement to, Lear. It has been said that
he is the passive complement to King Lear:

One tragic character imposes error, the other accepts it.
The roles continue consistently throughout the play—Lear
as active, Gloucester as passive.[21]

Looking at it from the point of view of the Elizabethan
idea of human nature, the Earl can be interpreted as an aspect
of the sensitive soul. According to Elizabethan psychology,
man has three souls—the vegetable, the sensible and the
rational. Of these, the sensible soul is the one he shares with
the lower animals. The chief function of this soul is to
motivate man to action by the stimulation of affection and
passion. According to Erasmus, there are two "masterless
tyrants" that hinder our reason—anger and lust. It has been
inferred that it is these two aspects of the sensible soul which
Lear and Gloucester respectively represent:

...identifying in Lear and Gloucester the traditional aspects
of the sensitive soul: the irascible and the concupiscible
matching the protagonists' anger and lechery.[22]

This interpretation is based on the fact that Lear is easily
angered and the Earl had indulged in licentious love which
resulted in the birth of Edmund. Edgar tells Edmund:

The Gods are just, and of our pleasant vices
Make instruments to plague us;
The dark and vicious place where thee he got
Cost him his eyes.[23]

There is also the viewpoint of Absurdism. From this point
of view King Lear has much that is comic and grotesque about
it (Vide Chapter 2, the section on Genre, supra). The analysis
from this point of view stresses the meaningless cruelty that life
itself metes out to human beings which also has a comic side
to it. About Gloucester this critic says:

The blind Gloucester, who has climbed a non-existent
heights and fallen on flat boards, is a clown.[24]

(d) Edmund

Edmund is the villain of the play—a Machiavellian character. He is also a malcontent, i.e., man who is deeply frustrated for having been subjected to injuries through no fault of his own. Such characters are very common in Elizabethan plays and most of the time the malcontent is also a Machiavellian villain whose plotting and intriguing bring about the downfall of the hero.

In Edmund's case it has to be noted that though he imagines himself to be ill-used, this is not actually the case. His father loves him, perhaps a little more than he loves Edgar and takes him to Court and specially recommends him to Kent. Yet Edmund cannot accept the fact that he is illegitimate and has a grudge against Edgar. This is because Edgar is not only the legitimate but the first-born son of the Earl, and as such will inherit Gloucester's title and land. Though Edmund will not be deprived, yet he wants more than his fair share—he wants all the privileges that are Edgar's birthright. So he plots the downfall of Edgar and is eminently successful in his intentions.

The note of dissatisfaction, ambition and hypocrisy is clearly struck in the very beginning. As soon as he enters the stage in the second scene he makes his attitude clear in a soliloquy:

> For that I am some twelve or fourteen moon-shines
> Lag of a brother? Why bastard? Wherefore base?
> ...   .
> Well, my legitimacy, if this letter speed,
> And my invention thrive, Edmund the base
> Shall top th' legitimate: I grow, I prosper;
> Now, gods, stand up for bastards![25]

He knows that he is as clever, if not cleverer than, his brother and he regards his father as a fool. He knows that Edgar's nature is so noble that he will never suspect him of villainy and his father is too credulous to doubt his allegations against Edgar. He, therefore, feels secure in his villainy and proceeds to weave his plots.

He makes his father believe in Edgar's supposed villainy by producing the forged letter and later pretending to have been wounded by him. Thus, with efficient ease, he gets rid of Edgar and is now sure of inheriting the title and property of the Ear!. Yet this is not enough for him. He has great resentment against Gloucester and his support of King Lear gives Edmund the excuse for betraying him:

> This courtesy, forbid thee, shall the Duke
> Instantly know: and of that letter too.[26]

Thus he gets his father arrested for a traitor, blinded and driven out like a beggar. Villainy triumphs.

He at once succeeds to the title and property of his father, but even this is not enough. His star rises even higher, for Goneril is attracted to him and makes advances. She gives him a love-token and kisses him. In the same scene we come to know that Cornwall has died. Regan, a widow now, wants to marry Edmund. She tells Oswald:

> My lord is dead; Edmund and I have talk'd
> And more convenient is he for my hand
> Than for your lady's.[27]

Realising that both the sisters want him, Edmund wavers between the two:

> Which of them shall I take?
> Both? One? Or neither? Neither can be enjoy'd
> If both remain alive.[28]

In other words, he does not love any of them. He is incapable of loving anybody. The only person he loves is his own self. Cold-bloodedly he plots that Albany would be killed by one of the sisters and then he would become the King of England.

So long as Lear and Cordelia are alive he cannot become the king, so he prepares to kill both of them. The two sisters however are so violently jealous of each other that they quarrel in front of him. By this time Albany has read the letter given him by Edgar and he challenges Edmund to prove his innocence. Edmund, however villainous he might be, is at least a brave

man and is ready to fight. Unfortunately, it is Edgar, the man
who has all the reason to detest him, answers the challenge
and wounds him.

For the first time his luck forsakes him and the wound
Edgar gives him is a death-wound. Now there comes a change
of heart in him. When Edgar reveals his identity he accepts the
verdict of fate:

> Thou hast spoken right, 'tis true
> The wheel has come full circle; I am here.[29]

As he comes to know of the death of both the sisters and
knows that he himself is at the point of death, he decides to
undo some of the wrongs he had done and try to save Lear
and Cordelia. This is his last action.

Edmund is thus presented as an unmitigated villain at first,
but at the last moment undergoes a change of heart and partly
redeems himself. He has been called the "wittiest and most
attractive of villains" by Wilson Knight. This critic also
considers him to be a tragic hero, the only proper tragic hero
in the play:

> Edmund alone steers something of an unswerving tragic
> course, brought to a fitting, deserved, but spectacular end,
> slain by his wronged brother, nobly repentant at the last.[30]

Not all critics would agree with this view, for, according
to all, Lear remains the undisputed hero of the play.

(e) Edgar

Just as Edmund is evil, so is Edgar a totally good character.
The two brothers complement each other. Paradoxically, it is
Edmund who gives the best description of Edgar:

> ...a brother noble
> Whose nature is so far from doing harms
> That he suspects none, on whose foolish honesty
> My practice rides easy.[31]

Edgar proceeds to fulfill the expectations that this
description rouses in the mind of the reader. He has implicit
faith in Edmund and does whatever he says. Thus, hearing his
name being proclaimed as that of a traitor, he decides to

disguise himself. He is the second character in the play to do so.

This disguise has itself given rise to many speculations among critics. Many of them cannot accept it and say it is not necessary. Edmund, however, explains right in the beginning the necessity for it:

> No port is free, no place,
> That guard, and most unusual vigilance
> Does not attend my taking.[32]

Thus the disguise itself is justified, but why he chooses the disguise of a ragged madman is not explained. Moreover, though he is racked by pity when he sees the plight of his father, he does not reveal himself and this has been listed as one of the improbabilities of the play by Bradley:

> Why does Edgar not reveal himself to his blind father, as he truly says he ought to have done? The answer is left to mere conjecture.[33]

His disguise is so successful that his father does not recognise him by his voice, whether as Poor Tom or later, after his attempted suicide, as a peasant. This impenetrability of his disguise has also been considered as one of the weaknesses of the play.

Exactly when Edgar begins to lose faith in Edmund and suspect his villainy is not made clear. The first time when we have an indication of this is when he fights Oswald. He finds the letter, written by Goneril to Edmund. Here also he blames Goneril more than Edmund and it is very doubtful whether he realises the extent of Edmund's villainy. When, however, he comes in answer to the herald's proclamation, he makes it clear that he knows everything:

> ...thou art a traitor,
> False to thy gods, thy brother and thy father,
> Conspirant 'gainst this high illustrious prince.[34]

In personal temper, his optimism is set against his father's pessimism. Whenever Gloucester sounds the note of despair, Edgar counters it by affirming faith. There are two places in the play in particular when this becomes noticeable. After he has saved Gloucester from committing suicide he tells him:

> Think that the clearest Gods, who make them honours
> Of men's impossibilities, have preserved thee.[35]

But the most important example of stoicism to be found in Shakespeare comes later, in the field of battle. He makes Gloucester stand under a tree and Gloucester says, on a note of despair: "a man may rot even here." Then Edgar counters:

> Men must endure
> Their going hence, even as their coming hither:
> Ripeness is all.[36]

It is this stoicism keeping his head unbowed though bloody, that has earned him the honour of delivering the epilogue of the play:

> The weight of this sad time we must obey:
> Speak what we feel, not what we ought to say
> The oldest hath borne most: we that are young
> Shall never see so much, nor live so long.[37]

(f) The Fool

There are many "fools" or "clowns" to be found in Elizabethan plays, but Shakespeare's "fools" are a class by themselves. Lear's Fool, specially, is a character almost unique.

Many kinds of fools are to be found in contemporary plays—the city gull, the country gull, the professional clown etc. Since comedy deals with follies and vices, fools abound in them, but they are present in tragedies as well. Shakespeare's Fools stand out, particularly Feste in the comedy of *Twelfth Night* and Lear's Fool in the tragedy of *King Lear*.

Whether at Court or in society, clowns occupied an important place. They had more freedom of speech than anyone else. They were professional entertainers at whose head was the Court Jester, who was a well-known figure in society. Will Summers for example, was the Court Fool of King Henry VIII. He had become so well-known a figure that Nashe wrote a play about him. Lear is an affectionate master to his Court Jester.

Robert Armin was a clown-actor and had joined Shakespeare's company to enact the roles of clowns. He was a man of such superior capacities that after he joined the troupe Shakespeare started to create more and more complex Fools. Prior to him there was Will Kempe who sang as well as danced:

> In 1599 he left and it was then that Shakespeare met the congenial Robert Armin for whom he created Touchstone, Feste, the grave-diggers in *Hamlet*, and the Fool in *King Lear*.[38]

Armin was proud of his learning and had written a book of quips and jests. Many of Shakespeare's quips are taken from this book. He himself was a "wise fool" and not just a low-grade entertainer. Lear's Fool was a character whom he could portray effectively and, seeing his capacities, Shakespeare could create a clown who would rise above mere clowning.

Lear's Fool is the most important Fool in Shakespeare and one of the most important characters in this play. Usually Fools are regarded as minor characters, but Feste in *Twelfth Night* and Lear's Fool are major ones. Enid Welsford has given his portrait in a nutshell:

> Shakespeare makes the fullest possible use of the accepted conventions that it is the Fool who speaks the truth, which he knows not by ratiocination but by inspired intuition.[39]

Thus Lear's Fool continues to tell him how unwise he had been in trusting his elder daughters. In this play the Fool appears in six scenes only: Act I, sc. iv, sc. v; Act II, sc. iv; Act III, sc. i, sc. iv and sc. vi. In all these six scenes he tries indefatigably to bring Lear to a sense of his own folly. Telling him about it after the harm has already been done may seem to be useless, but it is not so from another point of view. He is trying to make Lear realise that though his daughters are definitely to be blamed, he himself cannot be exempted. Lear has been thinking of himself as a wronged and ill-used man, "more sinned against than sinning" and has been cursing his daughters. He has to be made to realise that much blame accrues to him also. It is only the Fool who is wise enough to realise this and he sets about doing this in his own way, by joking and singing. He calls Lear a fool quite openly, and that too a bitter fool:

> The sweet and bitter fool
> Will presently appear,
> The one in motley here
> The other found out there.[40]

Taking the implication in, Lear asks him: "Dost thou call me fool, boy?" and the Fool comes out with one of his wisest sayings:

> All thy other titles thou hast given away; that thou wert born with.[41]

In other words, this means that all the other titles of Lear as the King were given to him by society, but his folly was an inborn attribute. But Lear is deaf to these sayings he takes them as part of a jester's attempts to entertain. We have to remember that at the time of this dialogue the King has just come in from hunting and does not yet know what is in store for him.

When he decides to go to Regan, the Fool tries to warn him, but Lear is so taken up with the ingratitude of Goneril that he does not pay any heed. Then after the terrible scene with the two daughters he goes out and the Fool is the only one with him in this storm scene. Lear is raving against his daughters. The Fool tells him to swallow his pride and go to his daughters but Lear hardly hears him. Finally, he sings the extremely significant quatrain that has been echoed in Feste's last song in *Twelfth Night*:

> He that has a little tiny wit,
>   With hey, ho, the wind and the rain,
> Must make content with his fortunes fit.
>   Tho' the rain it doth raineth every day.[42]

This gets Lear's attention at last, for he says: "True, boy".

After this the Fool delivers a speech in couplets, remarking on the state of the world in general. This is an intriguing speech, for half of it refers to the present situation and the next half to a Utopian state of honesty and prosperity. The second part is hopeful:

> When priests are more in words than matter;
> When brewers mar their malt with water;
> ... ...
> Nor squire in debt, nor no poor knight
> When slanders do not live in tongues;
> Not cut-purses come not to throngs.[43]

The entire speech is supposed to be a prophecy by Merlin. The Fool brings the harrowing scene to a close with this prophecy, declaring in a provocative manner:

> This prophecy Merlin shall make; for I
> Live before his time.[44]

In other words he has adopted the persona of a mage living before Merlin and this has intrigued the critics.

In the Mock trial-scene, realising that Lear is now mad, he indulges his whims as, indeed, Edgar also does. Just before the second entrance of Gloucester with the litter to take Lear to Dover, he says in a short and ambiguous sentences: "And I'll go to bed at noon"[45]

These are his last words in the play and it has been pointed out that this sentence can be understood in seven different ways, one of them being a proverbial prophecy about his own death, for "bed" can mean "grave".[46]

Tolstoy had objected to the presence of the Fool and deemed it unnecessary. This view is an extreme one and is not shared by other critics. The Fool is extremely necessary, though he appears only in six scenes:

> The Fool is integral to the play. He acts not only as a sort of chorus, making the central situation clearer by commenting on it more intelligently than the other characters, but as a foil to Lear's frenzies.[47]

There are, indeed, many interpretations of the Fool's character, for he is by far the sanest person in the play. Some of these are:

> Enid Welsford: The impartial critic, the mouthpiece of real sanity.

Northrop Frye: A much shrewder person than Oswald, representing something still unspoiled and innocent in the midst of a fallen nature.

Jan Kott: In *King Lear* it is the Fool who deprives majesty of its sacredness.[48]

(g) Cordelia

Cordelia has been justly looked upon as goodness personified. Her dignity, her self-respect, her honesty, her love—all these go to make her a character who is the very embodiment of positive ideals.

Her refusal to gratify her father's spoken and unspoken demands in the love-test can be understood in various ways. On one hand, it can be seen as eloquent testimony to her disgust at her sisters' hypocrisy and her own honesty. After listening to Goneril she says:

What shall Cordelia speak? Love, and be silent.[49]

Later, as Lear importunes her, she stands firm in her integrity. When threatened with loss of her portion of the kingdom, she still will not flatter. Nor does she deviate by so much as a hair's breadth when the Duke of Burgundy withdraws his suit. In other words, she renounces worldly wealth, power and security in favour of honesty and truthfulness.

But, equally well, there can be another approach to this refusal. It can be said that there is too much of inflexibility in her; that she is unkind and obstinate in refusing to please her father; that in her obstinacy she is being her father's daughter. There are quite a few critics who are of this opinion. Thus, pointing to the failure of the scheme of a love-test, Bradley says:

We may even say that the main cause of its failure was not that Goneril and Regan were exceptionally hypocritical, but that Cordelia was exceptionally sincere and unbending.[50]

It is not just Lear's folly that brings about his downfall

but Cordelia is also, to a certain extent, responsible for it. This view is shared by G. Wilson Knight:

> Cordelia cannot subdue her instinct to any judgement advising tact rather than truth.[51]

The same view had been expressed much earlier by Coleridge. It has been suggested, also, that the different traits of Lear's character have become diffused in his children:

> Lear may be said sequentially to dissociate in his children, Goneril and Regan (self-willfulness), and Cordelia (courageous adamancy).[52]

It is usual, however, to look upon her as almost a symbol of love and nobility of soul. Thus, mentioning her "heavenly beauty of soul" A.W. Schlegel compares her with Sophocles's Antigone, and G. Wilson Knight describes "the white innocence and resplendent love-strength of Cordelia." There are those who give a religious interpretation of the play and they look upon Cordelia as a symbolic figure who descends upon a world of evil:

> Divine Love, symbolised by Cordelia, enters a kingdom already divided against itself.[53]

Just as Lear is the tragic hero of the play, Cordelia is his female counterpart. She too makes an error of judgement when she deliberately fails the love-test, and is disinherited. She marries the King of France and goes off with him to lead what can be supposed to be a happy domestic life but tragic doom overtakes her in spite of everything. She is killed at the end of the play—a death that is not only unnecessary but a horrible one. Dr. Johnson's reaction to her death is well-known. He was so shocked by it that for many years he was not able to read the play again. G.W. Knight expresses the views of the modern reader:

> ...the ending of Cordelia is horrible, cruel, unnecessarily cruel—the final grotesque horror in the play.[54]

As a dramatic character, however, Cordelia is not as complex as Lear or the Fool, for Shakespeare has not presented as many different facets of her personality. We know that she is a "good character" and when she refuses to gratify Lear, it is perhaps the only time that she disobeys him. We also know that there is absolutely no rancour in her heart, for when in the reunion-scene Lear says that he had given her cause for resentment. She is so moved that she can hardly speak and just murmurs "No cause, no cause." When she is imprisoned all her thoughts are for her father, not for herself:

> For thee, oppressed King. I am not cast down;
> Myself could else out-frown false Fortune's frown.[55]

We also know that her love is not meant only for her father but extended to others, humbler persons also. Only once indirect mention is made of this, for we are told that the Fool had pined away after her departure. This argues that she had been kind and loving to this man who is hardly given any importance by the other courtiers. Shakespeare has created one of his most impressive characters in her.

(h) Kent

The Earl of Kent is the last of the major characters in the play, though, in the list of the *Dramatis Personae* his is the name next to Lear's, separated by those of many minor characters. This list, of course, made in order of social importance, so the names of kings and of dukes come before those of Earls. Social importance, however, is not the same as dramatic importance.

Like Edgar, Kent is a character who is entirely "good"—honest and loyal. Coleridge's comment still remains the best:

> Kent is the nearest to perfect goodness of all Shakespeare's characters and the most individualistic.[56]

This goodness and individualism first becomes apparent when he protests against Lear's injustice to Cordelia. He is the only one in the crowded court who dares protest. He has but only addressed the King when Lear stops him with the terrible words:

> Come not between the dragon and his wrath.[57]

But this does not deter Kent and at the risk of incurring the King's displeasure he tries to dissuade him. He is so perturbed that he does not mince words and calls Lear old, mad, and a fool and advises him to be more controlled:

> Reserve thy state;
> And in thy best consideration, check
> This hideous rashness.[58]

The King knows his honesty and his undoubted loyalty and tells him to shut up but Kent does not do so. He clearly invites his own misfortune. This destructive outspokenness is his only fault. Truly speaking, his rash words would be resented by anyone except somebody who is his inferior. It is not surprising that he is upbraided and banished on pain of death.

Thus, after having revealed him as an honest and frank man who is a bit too outspoken, the dramatist next shows him as a man whose loyalty can be held up as an example. Instead of being resentful of his banishment Kent adopts the disguise of Caius the servant and joins Lear's retinue. He is desperately anxious for Lear and his only thought is to serve him:

> Now, banish'd Kent
> If thou canst serve where thou dost stand condemned
> So may it come, thy master, whom thou lov'st
> Shall find thee full of labour.[59]

This is the scene in which Goneril insults Lear who decides to leave her and go to Regan. So Kent is sent ahead to inform Regan.

Here also his hot-headedness earns him imprisonment in the stocks. He offends and beats Oswald. He is very like Lear in his rashness. What happens after he is set free is not very clear for he is not mentioned in the rest of the scene. Whether he goes out with the King is not made clear. Perhaps not, because in the next scene he asks a Gentleman about the King which he would not have done if he had been with the King all the time. He sends the Gentleman as a messenger to Cordelia. Then come the harrowing storm-scenes in which he, the Fool and Poor Tom are with the King. He sees the King going mad in front of his eyes and cannot do anything except humour him and try to keep him calm. He succeeds in finally persuading the King to lie down and go to sleep just before Gloucester comes.

We see him next talking to the Gentleman he had sent to Cordelia and so we come to know how she had received the news about the King. Then a few scenes later we see him telling the whole history of Lear's tribulations to Cordelia. Even now he refuses to reveal himself to Lear and this has been pointed out as one of the improbabilities of the play by A.C. Bradley. These conversations of Kent with the gentleman and Cordelia serve to keep the audience informed about Cordelia's own arrival to rescue Lear. In this same scene, after the holy re-union of Cordelia and Lear there is again a dialogue between Kent and a Gentleman which brings the news up to date.

We see him next in the last scene. He is in time to see the terrible scene in which Lear enters with Cordelia's dead body. Now he at last reveals himself to Lear, when it is already too late. With Lear's death he loses all impetus to live. Thus when Albany requests him and Edgar to rule jointly in England he can only say:

> I have a journey, sir, shortly to go;
> My master calls me, I must not say no.[60]

He remains a loyal servant to the end. How can he refuse to follow Lear in the other world when he had spent his life following him in this world?

Kent is also important from a functional point of view. It is he who is in regular contact with Cordelia and informs her of the treachery of the two sisters and the consequent events. He, more than any other character, serves as a channel for the news that has to be conveyed to the readers.

REFERENCES

1. Quoted by Fluchère, Henri, *op. cit.*, p. 131.
2. Butcher, S.H., *Aristotle's Theory of Poetry and Fine Art with a Critical Text Translation of 'The Poetics'*. New Delhi: Kalyani Pubs., 1981, p. 53.
3. *Ibid.*, p. 53.
4. Fluchère, H., *op. cit.*, p. 136.

5. Butcher, *op. cit.*, p. 45.
6. *Ibid.*, p. 57.
7. *Ibid.*, pp. 45-47.
8. *Ibid.*, p. 45.
9. Bradley, A.C., *op. cit.*, p. 232.
10. Heilman, Robert B., *The Unity of King Lear*, in Kermode, *op. cit.*, p. 171.
11. Act III, sc. iv, ll. 32-36, p. 108.
12. Act IV, sc. viii, ll. 59-63, p. 179.
13. Act IV, sc. viii, line 84, p.180.
14. Kermode, F., *op. cit.*, pp. 32, 39, 44, 81, 120 respectively.
15. Knight, G.W., *op. cit.*, p. 131.
16. Act IV, sc. i, ll. 19-24, p. 139.
17. Act I, sc. ii, ll. 100-101, p. 28.
18. Act IV, sc. i, ll. 36-37, p. 140.
19. Act IV, sc. vi, ll. 75-77, p. 162.
20. Act V, sc. iii, ll. 195-98, p. 198.
21. Heilman, R., *op. cit.*, p. 173.
22. Elton, W.R., *op. cit.*, p. 245.
23. Act V, sc. iii, ll. 169-72, p. 197.
24. Kott, Jan, *King Lear or Endgame*, in Kermode, *op. cit.*, p. 275.
25. Act I, sc. ii, ll. 5-22, pp. 23-24.
26. Act III, sc. iii, ll. 21-22, p. 106.
27. Act IV, sc. v, ll. 30-32, pp. 157-58.
28. Act V, sc. i, ll. 57-59, pp. 184-85.
29. Act V, sc. iii, ll. 172-73, p. 197.
30. Knight, G. Wilson, *op. cit.*, p. 133.
31. Act I, sc. ii, ll. 176-79, p. 32.
32. Act II, sc. iii, ll. 3-5, p. 76.
33. Bradley, A.C., *op. cit.*, p. 211.
34. Act V, sc. iii, ll. 132-34, p. 195.
35. Act IV, sc. vi, ll. 73-74, p. 162.
36. Act V, sc. ii, ll. 9-11, p. 186.
37. Act V, sc. iii, ll. 332-35, p. 206.
38. Bradbrook, M.C., *Robert Armin and Twelfth Night,* in Palmer, D., ed., *Twelfth Night: A Casebook.* London: Macmillan, 1972, p. 223.
39. Welsford, E., *The Fool in King Lear*, in Kermode, *op. cit.*, p. 147.
40. Act I, sc. iv, ll. 141-44, p. 41.

41. Act I, sc. iv, ll. 146-47, p. 41.
42. Act III, sc. ii, ll. 70-74, p. 104.
43. Act III, sc. ii, ll. 81-88, p. 105.
44. Act III, sc. ii, ll. 95-96, p. 105.
45. Act III, sc. vi, line 83, p. 128.
46. Muir, K., *op. cit.*, p. 128, footnote.
47. Orwell, G., *Lear, Tolstoy and the Fool*, in Kermode, *op. cit.*, p. 157.
48. Kermode, *op. cit.*, pp. 147, 266 and 290 respectively.
49. Act I, sc. i, line 61, p. 7.
50. Bradley, A.C., *op. cit.*, pp. 86-87.
51. Knight, G.W., *op. cit.*, p. 119.
52. Elton, W.R., *Double Plot in King Lear*, in Kermode, *op. cit.*, p. 256.
53. Kermode, *op. cit.*, p. 191.
54. Knight, G.W., *op. cit.*, p. 133
55. Act V, sc. iii, ll. 5-6, p. 187.
56. Kermode, *op. cit.*, p. 39.
57. Act I, sc. i, line 121, p. 11.
58. Act I, sc. i, ll. 148-50, p. 12.
59. Act I, sc. iv, ll. 4-7, p. 34.
60. Act V, sc. iii, ll. 320-21, p. 206.

8

The Minor Characters

Unlike the other dramatists of his time Shakespeare took pains over the delineation of his minor characters as well as, and in addition to, his major ones. Even if a character comes on the stage very briefly, yet within that limited time Shakespeare depicts him in a convincing and concrete manner—he becomes an individual. Many of his minor characters are delineated as carefully as the important characters of other writers. In this play Lear is such an overwhelming character that all other characters are cast into the shade. Yet it has to be affirmed that they are individuals.

The positioning of the minor characters in *King Lear* is misleading. In the *Dramatis Personae,* the names of many minor characters come just after Lear's and before those of four other major characters. This is because the list is made in accordance with the social status of the characters. Thus kings are superior to dukes and dukes are superior to earls. The names of the earls of Kent and Gloucester therefore come lower than those of the Dukes of Burgundy, Cornwall and Albany, while that of the Fool comes very low indeed. In the ensuing discussion the same order shall be followed.

(a) The King of France

This character comes only in the first scene and that too in the latter part. He, however, leaves the impression of a character who is himself noble and values nobility in others. Though Cordelia is powerless and disowned by her father, he gladly accepts her:

> Fairest Cordelia, that art most rich, being poor;
> Most choice, forsaken; and most lov'd, despis'd!
> Thee and thy virtues here I seize upon.[1]

After this he goes back to his kingdom with her and is not seen any more. Later in the play, moved by Cordelia's distress at the news sent by Kent, he comes with his army to England in order to rescue Lear. This is made clear by Cordelia:

> My mourning and importun'd tears hath pitied.
> No blown ambition doth our arms incite.[2]

He has to go away to France on urgent business leaving his army and Cordelia in the hands of his Marshall, but it should not be forgotten that he had come on a charitable mission. He gains nothing out of it and, on the other hand, loses his beloved queen. In the little time he has been present on the stage he serves the important function of taking Cordelia away from England with all honour and leaves the impression of a man of nobility and integrity, of a soul above material gains. He is the perfect foil to the Duke of Burgundy for whom worldly gains are the be-all and the end-all of life. He gives the impression of being a man of sterling virtues, a fit mate for Cordelia.

(b) The Duke of Burgundy

This character who, like the King of France, is a suitor of Cordelia, is the opposite of the King. He withdraws his suit as soon as he finds that Lear has disinherited Cordelia. He has no regard for Cordelia herself.

> I am sorry, then, you have so lost a father
> That you must lose a husband.[3]

This is the last we see of him. He serves the purpose of being a foil to the King of France and leaves the impression of being a mercenary man.

(c) The Duke of Cornwall

Just as the King of France and the Duke of Burgundy stand as contrasts to each other so do the two Dukes of Cornwall and Albany. Cornwall is the very spirit of evil as opposed to Albany's goodness.

He is present in the first scene but does not speak. We see him next in Act II, sc. i, where he, along with Regan comes on a visit to the Earl of Gloucester. At first he seems to be a good administrator. It is true that he believes in whatever Gloucester and Edmund tell him of Edgar, but after all they are the father and the brother of Edgar. Edmund appears to him to be a loyal son and so he takes on Edmund as one of his trusted followers.

When he sees Kent and Oswald fighting in the next scene he does his best to find out the cause for the quarrel and it seems to him that Kent is in the wrong. Here some inkling of his nature is given when he puts Kent in the stocks. No doubt is left of his true nature in the next scene in which Lear meets Regan. He does not speak much but nor does he upbraid her. Lear, along with Gloucester, the Gentleman and the Fool are driven out in the impending storm and he, by not objecting, lends tacit support to Regan. At the end of the scene he orders Gloucester to close the doors, though Gloucester tells him that there is no shelter nearby for the King:

Shut up your doors, my lord; 'tis a wild night:
My Regan counsels well. Come out o'th'storm.[4]

The evil in his nature is fully revealed in the blinding-scene. It is he who puts out Gloucester's eyes, and when one of the loyal servants of the Earl wounds him the reader does not feel any sympathy for him. After this we do not see him and only hear of his death. No one mourns him, least of all his wife. He, like Edmund, is presented as an unmitigated villain.

(d) The Duke of Albany

This character balances Cornwall's evil and also the evil embodied in his wife, Goneril. He is a quiet and peace-loving character and at first does not concern himself with Goneril's doings. He shows himself as a weak character in Act I, sc. iv, and upbraids his wife very mildly for her treatment of Lear. Even then, this is a pointer to the goodness inherent in him, for he does upbraid her, though it comes rather late.

He starts taking an active part in the play from Act IV,

sc. ii onwards, strongly rebuking Goneril for her inhuman
attitude to Lear:

> O God!
> You are not worth the dust which the rude wind
> Blows in your face.[5]

He then reveals his nature as a man of honour and integrity
and also with a philosophical streak in him. He is an intellectual,
able to reach the general from the particular, the abstract from
the concrete:

> Humanity must perforce prey on itself,
> Like monsters of the deep.[6]

The added stimulant of the news of Gloucester's blinding that
Regan's messenger brings him awakens his princely valour and
justice:

> Gloucester, I live
> To thank thee for the love thou showd'st the king
> And to revenge thine eyes.[7]

After this he leads the English army in the battle and
Edmund leads the Duke of Cornwall's army. When the British
army wins it is to be noticed that he does not think of himself
as the King. To him it is Lear who is the King. Then in front
of him the two sisters quarrel shamelessly over Edmund, and
by this time he has also read Goneril's letter which incriminates
Edmund. Then, like a true knight he challenges Edmund as a
traitor when he could have easily arrested and punished him as
such. He is palpably the leader now and when, after the death
of Goneril, Regan, Lear and Cordelia he realises that he is the
heir to the kingdom, he is ready to renounce it in favour of
others. It is quite clear that he does not want to be the king,
but if he is forced to assume the responsibility he will rule
wisely and well. Shakespeare has presented a man who is
worthy of respect in the figure of the Duke of Albany.

(e) Curan

Curan is described as "a courtier" and is seen only once in
the play, in the first scene of Act II. The setting is the castle of
Gloucester where Edmund and Curan meet. He serves the

purpose of informing Edmund and the audience that the Duke
of Cornwall and Regan are going to come on a visit and that
they will arrive that very night. This affords Edmund the
opportunity to further his plot against Edgar.

Curan therefore serves just as a messenger. He also conveys
the rumour that there might be a battle between the Dukes of
Cornwall and Albany. This of course is a baseless rumour and
will not be referred to again.

Thus, though Curan is a very minor character and speaks
only nine lines in prose, he conveys an important news to
Edmund, Shakespeare's characters, for however short a time
they may come on the stage, are always functional characters,
as seen here.

(f) Oswald

This is one of the important minor characters of the play.
He is Goneril's steward and she trusts him implicitly. He is an
evil character though the evil in him is far weaker than in
Edmund and others. He is but a typical servant and a yes-man
who supports Goneril whole-heartedly. We see him for the
first time in Act I, sc. iii, where he is reporting to her how Lear
had struck one of her attendants who had scolded Lear's Fool.
She then directs him to be insolent to the King and neglect
him. He carries out this order, then towards the end of the
scene she sends him to Regan with a letter.

So far we have seen him as an obedient servant. When we
see him next he is alone and another facet of his character is
revealed. He has come to the castle of Gloucester and meets
Kent who is disguised as Caius before he has entered the
castle. He does not recognise Kent, but Kent recognises him
and insults him. The two start fighting when the Duke of
Cornwall comes in. Oswald tells him what has happened and
it is noticeable that he reports facts without misrepresenting
them.

He comes on the stage with Goneril in Act II, sc. iv, but
does not speak, and is next seen when he gives Cornwall and
the others the news of how the Earl of Gloucester has sent the
King to Dover. He next brings the news in Act IV, sc. ii, of

how the attitude of Albany has turned against Goneril. He is puzzled that Albany's reactions are so unexpected and says:

> What most he should dislike seems pleasant to him,
> What like, offensive.[8]

It is noticeable that here he uses his own intelligence and interprets Albany's attitude, thus serving to put Goneril on her guard.

In Act IV, sc. v, he has arrived at Gloucester's castle and has talked to Regan. He was going to Edmund with a letter from Goneril. Regan is a widow now and has her eyes on Edmund for a future husband. She asks him to desert Goneril and serve her. She also gives him a letter for Edmund or a love-token, it is not clear which. Oswald does not commit himself. He needs more time to make up his mind, but his answer to Regan is a model of diplomacy:

> Would I could meet him, madam: I should show
> What party I do follow.[9]

The answer satisfies Regan, though it is actually quite non-committal. It shows Oswald's devious mind.

The very next scene is his death-scene. This is the famous scene of Gloucester's attempted suicide. Oswald comes upon him and Edgar (who is now disguised as a peasant.). He is elated at finding Gloucester, for the latter carries a reward for his head. This joy is shortlived, for Edgar gives him his death-wound in no time. Even at the moment of death Oswald does not forget his duty and directs Edgar to take Goneril's letter from him and give it to Edmund.

Oswald is thus presented as an obedient and ideally dutiful servant with a streak of evil in him. He is a cunning, self-seeking opportunist who does not hesitate to kill the blind and helpless Gloucester in order to win the reward. In all, he is a distasteful man, but fully realistic.

(g) The Old Man

This character makes only a brief appearance in Act IV, sc. i, but leaves the impression of honesty, loyalty and goodness even within that short time. He has been the tenant of

Gloucester and his father for eighty years and is devoted to him. He leads blind Gloucester and has reached the heath where they meet Edgar. The Earl asks him to bring some clothes for Poor Tom who has only a blanket to cover him. The Old Man does not like to leave the Earl with a madman but is finally persuaded.

He then leaves the stage after having spoken only six and a half lines, but we know that he kept his promise for we see Edgar later dressed as a peasant.

Shakespeare has portrayed him as a man of few words, but as a man of his word. He is acting out of pure altruism in helping the Earl and thus leaves a lasting impression of goodness and generosity.

(h) The Gentleman

This Gentleman has been described as "attending on Cordelia" and appears in many important scenes. Kent sees him on the heath in Act III, sc. i. It is he who describes the King's condition to him in extremely graphic language:

> Contending with the fretful elements;
> Bids the wind blow the earth into the sea,
> Or swell the curled waters 'bove the main.[10]

Sensing his sympathy for Lear, Kent trusts him with a message for Cordelia which he willingly undertakes to deliver. We see him next in Act IV, sc. iii, again in conversation with Kent, near Dover. He tells how he had met Cordelia and describes her reaction to his news:

> She took them and read them in my presence,
> And now and then an ample tear trilled down
> Her delicate cheeks.[11]

This is a long conversation and at the end of the scene the Gentleman accompanies Kent to Lear. It is not known for sure whether he is the same Gentleman who comes upon Lear in his madness in Act IV, sc. vi, but perhaps he is. We see him again in the re-union scene and at the end of this scene he and Kent talk. This time it is Kent who gives him or rather confides in him the news of Cornwall's death, and how Edmund is

leading his army. In the last scene it is he who brings the news
of the death of Goneril and Regan, still holding the knife that
Goneril had used to commit suicide.

He is, thus, an extremely functional figure, bringing
important news to the main characters of the play, and at the
same time speaking powerful poetry. It is he who describes
Lear in the memorable lines:

> A sight most pitiful in the meanest wretch,
> Past speaking of in a king.[12]

(i) and (j) Goneril and Regan

These two are the feminine counterparts of Edmund and
Cornwall. Indeed one can hardly find their parallel either in
Shakespeare or in other dramatists of the time. They are of a
pair and there is nothing that can be said in mitigation of
either of them. Even Edmund repents at the end and tries to
undo the evil he has done, but these two sisters have nothing
to recommend them.

Goneril, being the eldest, is always in the lead. At first she
is shown as a hypocrite and an opportunist, professing her
non-existent love in extravagant terms. These are the first few
lines she speaks on the stage and the reader has been given no
hints about her character. But, with consummate artistry, the
poet has given her such hyperbolical language that the reader
cannot help thinking that something is wrong with such
vehement declarations:

> Dearer than eyes, space and liberty;
> Beyond what can be valued, rich or rare;
> No less than life, with grace, health, beauty, honour;
> As much as child e'er lov'd, or father found;
> A love that makes breath poor and speech unable;
> Beyond all manner of so much I love you.[13]

Regan, professing her love, goes a step further in spite of
Goneril's exaggerations:

> I profess
> Myself an enemy to all other joys
> Which the most precious spirit of sense possesses

> And find I am alone felicitate
> In your dear highness's love.[14]

Such extravagance almost presupposes hypocrisy and this
hypocrisy becomes apparent as soon as the two of them are
left together at the end of the scene.

Hypocrisy and insincerity, unfortunately, are not all. Soon
enough cruelty joins them. Goneril insults her father and takes
away half of his retinue. She forces him to go to Regan even
before he has stayed for one month with her, as he had
planned to do. She herself reaches Regan just as Lear is talking
to her. She unites with Regan in driving their father out of the
castle of Gloucester, in the storm.

Regan's cruelty is particularly highlighted in the blinding
of Gloucester. She plucks him by the beard and though it is
Goneril who first suggests the blinding, it is Regan who
remains throughout and supports her husband. It is Regan
who has him driven outside:

> Go thrust him out at gates and let him smell
> His way to Dover.[15]

As far as hypocrisy and cruelty are concerned, there is little
to choose between the two sisters. The same goes for the
sentiment of sinful love. Goneril candidly tells Edmund that
she despises her husband and favours him. Regan gets suspicious
and at the very first opportunity shamelessly declares him her
husband:

> Witness the world, that I create thee here
> My lord and master.[16]

They come to the miserable end they so richly deserve, for
Goneril poisons Regan and then kills herself. They can hardly
be paralleled for their wickedness. Maynard Mack is of the
opinion that it is this wickedness that is their reason for
existence:

> The fact that they are paradigms of evil rather than (or as
> well as) exasperated spoilt children whose patience has
> been exhausted gives them their stature and dramatic
> force.[17]

REFERENCES

1. Act I, sc.i, ll. 249-251, p. 19.
2. Act II, sc iv, ll. 26-27, p. 156.
3. Act I, sc.i, ll. 245-46, p. 19.
4. Act II, sc iv, ll. 306-07, p. 95.
5. Act IV, sc.ii, ll. 29-31, p. 145.
6. Act IV, sc.ii, ll. 48-49, p. 146.
7. Act IV, sc.ii, ll. 94-96, p. 150.
8. Act IV, sc.ii, ll. 10-11, p. 143.
9. Act IV, sc.v, ll. 39-40, p. 158.
10. Act III, sc.i, ll. 4-6, p. 96.
11. Act IV, sc.iii, ll. 11-13, p. 151.
12. Act IV, sc.vi, ll. 201-02, p. 171.
13. Act I, sc.i, ll. 55-60, p. 6.
14. Act I, sc.i, ll. 71-75, pp. 7-8.
15. Act III, sc.vii, ll. 91-92, p. 135.
16. Act V, sc.iii, ll. 78-79, p. 192.
17. Mack, M., *op. cit.*, p. 71.

9

The Plot-Structure

The plot, as Aristotle says, is "the soul of tragedy" and he lists it as the first of the six elements of tragedy. He had laid down many rules concerning the plot of a tragedy, which has been explained and added to by his commentators. The Elizabethans were fully conversant with them. Some of the basic ideas about the tragic plot as given by Aristotle shall now be explained.

(a) The Classical Rules

It is necessary, in this context, to keep Aristotle's definition of tragedy in mind:

> Tragedy, then, is an imitation of an action that is serious, complete, and of a given magnitude; in language embellished with each kind of artistic ornament, the several kinds being found in separate parts of the play; in the form of action, not of narrative; through pity and fear affecting the proper purgation of these emotions.[1]

It is not possible to explain the complexity of meaning in this definition, for it has many implications. The diligent student will treat this definition, as indeed the Elizabethan dramatists did, as a point of reference, for the rules that follow and the features that shall now be mentioned all hark back to it.

The most obvious and well-known are the rules of the Unities. There are three of them: (i) the Unity of Action, (ii) the Unity of Time, and (iii) the Unity of Place. It is a well-known fact that Shakespeare did not take these rules very seriously, for he rarely observed them.

(i) **The Unity of Action:** This is the most important of the rules and refers directly to the definition given above. Aristotle says that the action of a tragedy is "serious", and this rule implies that there should be no mingling of serious and trivial actions. This rule is specially meant for tragedies, for pity and terror, which are the emotions roused by serious action, are relegated to tragedies. Shakespeare does not observe this rule for in *King Lear* as well as in other tragedies there are frequent comic scenes. The Fool, in *King Lear*, is constantly trying to enliven the play by jesting and singing. His fooling, it is true, is no coarse entertainment for its own sake, but it exists.

(ii) **The Unity of Time:** Ideally, the time covered by the play should be just as much as is covered by the actual performance on the stage. Aristotle however, allows "a single revolution of the sun", i.e. the story of a play should take about a full day. This is difficult, but not impossible. Ben Jonson, for example, takes no more than a full day for his plays.

Shakespeare, it is well-known, does not care much about the rules. In the chronicle plays it is not possible to observe this rule, since such plays naturally take up a long span of time. As far as *King Lear* is concerned, it cannot be said with certainty how much time the play covers—definitely more than a month. Lear's travails start before his month with Goneril is over, though we do not know how long this period is. After this Kent sends news to Cordelia, then the King of France arrives at Dover with his army. After some days the battle is fought. All this would mean a month or more, though nothing can really be affirmed.

(iii) **The Unity of Place:** According to this all the action of the play should take place in one place only. It should, however, be borne in mind that Aristotle did not specifically recommend it. The idea came to the Elizabethan dramatists from that relies of the Italian Renaissance: Sialigvi Scaliger, Minturno, Castelvetro et al. who had misread Aristotle. Anyway, the unity of place as it was understood is very difficult to follow and the only Elizabethan dramatist who follows it is

Ben Jonson, though even in his plays all the scenes do not have the same location. Shakespeare did not follow it in *King Lear*. There are frequent changes of scenes (*Vide* Chapter 5, *A Scene-wise Summary, supra*). It is very rarely, indeed, that even two consecutive scenes are located in the same place. The neo-classical critics of his own time and of later times, had condemned Shakespeare for not observing these rules. One of the greatest neo-classical critics, Dr. Johnson, however, had defended him. The defence of the violation of this particular rule has become specially famous.

These and many other rules regarding the tragic plot had been laid down by Aristotle and explained by later scholars. One of them was Donatus, whose treatise on drama was prescribed for study in Elizabethan times. He has explained Aristotle's theory in detail and also added his own. According to him the first section of the play is Prologue. This is usually a short speech occurring before the actual action starts. Marlowe's Prologue to *Dr. Faustus*, is a very good example of a Prologue in the classical manner. Shakespeare too has written prologues to a few of his plays, but usually he incorporates them within the first scene of the play, as is the case with *King Lear*. The conversation between Gloucester and Kent before the entrance of the King and Court is in the nature of a Prologue.

There are certain other classical rules to be observed in writing a tragedy. *Peripeteia* or the reversal of fortune is such a device. It implies the fall of the hero from a high into a low status. This is clarified by Aristotle. Seeking to explain the ideal plot for a tragedy, he rejects three outlines and finally fixes on the plot that gives a rather good man coming from prosperity to adversity. Nowhere is *peripeteia* better illustrated than in *King Lear*. In the beginning we see him as a mighty man:

> When the play opens he is presented as in one sense a king of kings.[2]

Yet this "king of kings" then gradually falls so low as no other tragic hero has fallen. All other heroes retain their reason, however, low they might fall. Lear loses even that. He is indeed unique in this respect.

A very important part of the tragic plot is *Anagnorisis* or Recognition. This, at its crudest level, involves the mutual recognition of two characters who have been separated, as happens in *Twelfth Night* when Viola and Sebastian recognise each other. The most subtle recognition is that which occurs when a character recognises his own nature. This is the kind of recognition that occurs in *King Lear* and it occurs several times. Out on the heath, thinking of the poor who have no shelter he recognises his own neglect:

> O! I have ta'en
> Too little care of this. Take physic, pomp.[3]

Later, in the re-union scene, after he has recovered from his terrible madness he says:

> I am a very foolish fond old man,
> Fourscore and upward, not an hour more or less;
> And, to speak plainly,
> I fear I am not in my perfect mind.[4]

These ineffable lines take *anagnorisis* to its farthest extreme. It is difficult to find their parallel.

Another instance of Recognition in the play is Gloucester's recognition of Lear. It is true that he fails to recognise his own son, but he recognises Lear as soon as he hears the voice. Lear is fully mad now and cannot recognise Gloucester, but the latter knows him by his voice. Again, in the last scene Lear recognises Kent. A very important recognition takes place when Gloucester says, I stumbled then (Act IV, sc.i, 20). There are, thus, several instances of *anagnorisis*, throughout the play, of different levels of subtlety.

Another important part of the plot, listed by Aristotle after *Peripeteia* and *Anagnorisis*, is *Pathos* or the scene of Suffering. This comprises death, physical pain, etc. All tragedies must, of necessity, contain such scenes, and *King Lear* has these in full measure. The storm-scenes and the blinding of Gloucester at once spring to the mind.

(b) Certain Elizabethan Features

It is taken for granted that a tragedy should have but one plot. There might be intrigues, but a sub-plot goes against classical rules. They are permitted in comedies, particularly in the New Comedy, but not in tragedies. The use of more than one plot in a tragedy is an Elizabethan feature. As it is, the sub-plot is a comic one and this violates the unity of action. This, however, is not the case with *King Lear* as it is with Marlowe's *Dr. Faustus*, for here the sub-plot of Gloucester is not a comic one but repeats and reinforces the same theme as in the main plot.

It is a remarkable feature of Elizabethan plays that the several plots are not arbitrarily put into the play. Instead there is a definite relationship between the main plot and the sub-plot, whether there is but one, or several of them. This relationship can be of many kinds and has been studied in detail. As a matter of fact, it is difficult to find a play that has only one plot. All the plays of Ben Jonson, for example, are multiple-plotted or at least double-plotted. In Shakespeare's plays also, as in the other plays of the time, this feature is to be noted. He gives two or more plots and neatly welds them together. It had been thought that the fact of having two plots constitutes one of the weaknesses of *King Lear* but as we shall see in a later section of this chapter, this is not the present view of the literary critics.

Another important feature of Elizabethan plays is the use of impenetrable disguises. This is one of the most common features of Shakespearean plots. The use of disguises resulting in mistaken identity produces dramatic irony, laughter and complications of plot. Our dramatist uses this device repeatedly, right from his early plays. He disguises his female characters as well as the male ones. *King Lear* is, however, a tragedy, so here the convention of disguise is not used merely for the sake of dramatic irony or for complicating the plot. Here the function of disguise goes much deeper:

> In tragedies the effect is more often to add to the complexity of the emotional structure of the play.[5]

Two characters adopt disguises in the play—Kent and Edgar. Both of these disguises add substantially to the emotional intensity of the play. Kent's loyalty is highlighted at every step and is meant to be contrasted with the lack of loyalty in his daughters, his own flesh and blood. Edgar's disguise is explained as necessary for self-defence but there is no need for him to adopt the disguise of a madman, any disguise would have done equally well. There was no need, moreover, to maintain the disguise for so long, specially with his blind father. The disguise of a madman was adopted and maintained for so long, not for any dramatic reasons, but for artistic reasons, that is, because they add to the emotional intensity of the play as a whole. The fact that the audience knows that Edgar is not actually mad only adds to the horror of the situation in the storm-scenes.

Edgar actually adopts two disguises and the second occurs in the mock-suicide scene (Act IV, sc. vi). After Gloucester's failure to kill himself, Edgar appears to him in the guise of a peasant and this is how he remains till, before the duel, he reveals his identity to his father, which is not shown on the stage, but only reported by him. On the stage itself he reveals himself only after he has dealt the death-blow to Edmund during the duel in the last scene.

All these three disguises, after the manner of Elizabethan plays, are quite impenetrable. Not only does Lear fail to recognise Kent, Gloucester does not recognise his own son. This is highlighted all the more by the fact that in his blindness he recognises the King by his voice, but not Edgar. This has been criticised on the ground of being improbable, but it has to be remembered that Lear, though mad, is not in disguise, so it is allowed by realistic as well as stage-rules for Gloucester to recognise him. Edgar however, is in disguise and impenetrability of disguises was one of the theatrical conventions of the time. So his father does not know him.

(c) The Sources of *King Lear*

Nearly all of the dramatists of the time took the material for their plays from many different works already in existence.

Old plays, narrative poems, romances, histories and other documents were used to provide the story of the play. As far as Shakespeare is concerned the study of the sources from which he took his material for the plot has become an important branch of Shakespeare studies. It is highly instructive as well as illuminating to see how he selected the material from six or seven different sources, then rejected some, retained some, elaborated some and modified some in accordance with his needs. As far as *King Lear* is concerned Shakespeare had many sources to cull his material from. Some of those he may have used are listed below:

1. Three scenes from an old play *King Leir*.

2. Holinshed's *Chronicles*.

3. Book II, Canto X of Spenser's *Faerie Queene*.

4. Certain stanzas from *The Mirror for Magistrates*.

5. The story of the Paphlagonian King from Sir Philip Sidney's *Arcadia*.

6. Florio's translation of Montaigne's *Essays*.

The most important of these is the first, the old anonymous play of *King Leir*. This is a full-length play and Shakespeare made several significant changes in the plot to suit his requirements. All that happens in the first seven scenes of the old play has been given in just one scene – the opening one. The most significant of these changes is concerned with the ending, for in the old play the Gallian King invades Britain, defeats the English army and restores Leir to the throne. The play ends there and there is no mention of the death of Cordella. Moreover, Leir does not become mad and there is no sub-plot in this play.

The changes that Shakespeare has introduced unquestionably contributed to the excellence of his play. First of all, he changed the very genre of the play, for whereas the old one ends in happiness (with the restoration of Leir to the throne) Shakespeare makes his play a tragedy. He made several other changes that made his play immeasurably superior to the former one. One such short example is the re-union scene which, in Shakespeare, takes on a hushed, sacred quality. In the old play the King and Cordella go on kneeling and rising till the scene verges on comedy:

> Cordella: Thy loving daughter speaketh unto thee.
> *(she kneels)*
> Leir: O stand thou up, it is my part to kneele,
> And ask forgiveness for my former faults.
> *(he kneels)*
> Cordella: O if you wish I should enjoy my breadth,
> Dear father, rise, or I receive my death.
> *(he riseth)*
> Leir: Then I will rise, to satisfy your mind
> But kneel again, till pardon be resigned.
> *(he kneels)*[6]

This is not the end, for, a few lines later Leir rises and Cordella rises, then again he kneels and rises again and then Mumford, who had been with them, also kneels and rises. All these kneelings and risings not only rob the scene of its dignity, but brings it near to comedy. In Shakespeare, there is talk of kneeling, but there is no stage direction about it. It may also be noted from this brief example, that the play is in couplets, whereas we have blank verse in Shakespeare.

In Holinshed, Cordeilla commits suicide with a dagger which Shakespeare has changed to hanging. This naturally adds to the pathos of the event and saves Cordelia from the unforgiveable sin of suicide.

In Spenser also Cordelia commits suicide by hanging herself:

> And overcommon kept in prison long,
> Till weary of that wretched life herself she hung.[7]

Spenser gives the same spelling to Cordelia's name as in Shakespeare, which no other writer does. So it is thought that Shakespeare took the spelling of Cordelia's name and the idea of hanging from Spenser but changed suicide to murder.

Sidney's story in *Arcadia* supplied Shakespeare with the sub-plot. The outline of the story is given right in the beginning by Sidney:

This old man (whom I lead) was lately rightful Prince of this countiy of Paphlagonia, by the hard-hearted ungratefulness of a son of his, deprived not only of his kingdom (whereof no foreign forces were ever able to spoil him), but of his state.[8]

After this the full story follows in all its details.

Thus there are many changes that Shakespeare has introduced, and always the change contributes to the superior quality of his own work.

(d) The Plot of *King Lear*

The play has two plots – that of the King being the main plot and that of the Earl of Gloucester being the subsidiary one. As has been indicated above, he took the material for these two plots from fairly variegated sources and brought the two together. The theme of foolish parents and ungrateful children occurs in both and the two complement each other. This welding together shows great mastery over technique and yet there are many objections against the plot of *King Lear*. All these objections have been categorised by A.C. Bradley under the label of "defects" and "improbabilities". A glance at these will reveal all the necessary details of the plot of *King Lear*. The defects, in the order given by A.C. Bradley, are as follows:

(1) The mock-suicide of Gloucester.

(2) The love-test.

(3) The blinding of Gloucester.

(4) The unhappy ending.

(5) The double action.

Taking up the first of these, Bradley himself defends it on the ground of its general suitability to the over-all atmosphere of the play. *King Lear* has a very intense atmosphere and that which may appear incongruous in other settings and other plays can be accepted without demur in such a play as this:

The imagination and the feelings have been worked upon with such effect...that we are unconscious of the grotesqueness of the incident for common sense.[9]

Bradley defends the love-test also. Shakespeare has taken up a legend here and has softened the incident as much as possible, making it psychologically credible. Everything had already been decided from beforehand and the test itself is but a mere formality. It is, also, perfectly in keeping with Lear's own nature. The entire scene, moreover, is highly effective on the stage:

> This scene acts effectively, and to imagination the story is not at all incredible.[10]

The third defect listed by Bradley is the blinding of Gloucester. First of all this goes against the classical rules which specify that all violent actions should take place off-stage. The self-blinding of Oedipus and the suicide of Jocasta in Sophocles's play are the best examples of violent action taking place off-stage. Bradley agrees with the general critical condemnation of the action but defends it by saying that it is in keeping with the general mood of the play:

> Thus the blinding of Gloster belongs rightly to *King Lear* in its proper world of imagination; it is a plot upon *King Lear* as a stage-play.[11]

The unhappy ending of the play has outraged readers so much that Nahum Tate had, in his adaptation of the play, given it a happy ending. Dr. Johnson could scarcely bear to read it. The death of Cordelia and Lear violate the concept of poetic justice. Bradley also is horrified and, after long arguments, wishes for Lear.

> ...what Shakespeare himself might have given him—peace and happiness by Cordelia's fireside.[12]

According to Bradley, the most serious defect of the plot is the double-plot action. He points out that the sub-plot adds to the number of important characters, makes their actions expressly complicated and makes too many events crowd upon one another. This tires the reader emotionally and confuses him intellectually.

These are the outstanding defects of the play and though later on there have been many disputes and critics have argued much about them, the position has not changed in any significant way.

The same can be said about the "improbabilities" as given by Bradley. These are concerned mainly with the sub-plot and they are many:

(1) Why should Edgar write a letter to Edmund when they live in the same house?

(2) Gloucester does not recognise his own son's writing.

(3) Edgar is persuaded to avoid meeting his father.

(4) Why should Gloucester go all the way to Dover, merely to kill himself?

(5) After the mock-suicide Edgar speaks to him like a gentleman, then to Oswald in the peasant dialect and then to him again in the language of a gentleman and yet Gloucester is not surprised.

(6) Rumours about the French invasion come much too early.

(7) Lear says that fifty of his knights have been dismissed but Goneril had never mentioned this.

(8) Lear and Goneril both send messages to Regan, but instead of waiting for answer, follow hard upon the heels of the messenger.

(9) Why does not Edgar disclose his identity to his father?

(10) Why does not Kent reveal himself till at the very end of the play?

(11) Why does Burgundy get the first choice for Cordelia's hand? The King of France has as good a right.

(12) Why does Edmund try to save Lear and Cordelia when it is too late?

Bradley himself hints that the list could be longer. He comes to the conclusion that these improbabilities show that the dramatist is much more concerned with serious issues and these insignificant details were carelessly swept aside:

Shakespeare, set upon the dramatic effects of the great scenes and upon certain effects not wholly dramatic, was exceptionally careless of probability, clearness and consistency in smaller matters.[13]

These highly illuminating observations of Bradley serve to acquaint us with the basic features of the plot of *King Lear*. They have been commented upon, defended or refuted by many later critics, but very little has been added that is completely new or different.

Just as plot is the soul of tragedy, so is conflict the heart of tragedy. We get various types of conflict in this play—on the most superficial as well as on the subtlest level, within the small compass of an individual's heart as well as between two kingdoms.

On the most superficial level and the largest in scope is the battle between England and France. This comes at the end and sets the seal on the tragic outcome by making Edmund triumph which enables him to order the execution of Lear and Cordelia.

Much narrower in scope is the familial conflict in both the plots. The main plot shows conflict between father and daughter and the sub-plot shows conflict between father and son. Later in the play we have another kind of domestic conflict, for in the main plot sister turns against sister and in the sub-plot brother turns against brother on the open field of combat.

Yet all this is practically nothing compared to the conflict that rages in the heart of Lear and that of Gloucester. In Lear's case it is of such intensity that it unseats his reason and in Gloucester's case it destroys his faith and drives him to commit suicide. Thus this subtle conflict leads to chaos and to despair. As Theodore Spencer has described:

> Everything has turned loose, Lear's own passions, the fury
> of the elements, the lustful desires of Regan and Goneril,
> all are horrifyingly released from order.[14]

At another level, a philosophical one, there is conflict between Man and the Universe which has led *King Lear* to be labelled as a "cosmic drama". Here we see Lear battling alone against all that is reprehensible in man and nature. All these different kinds of conflict give this play an intensity and depth that can hardly be paralleled anywhere else.

Continuing his observations on the play, the same critic points out that the sub-plot is not, as A.C. Bradley had said, a mere repetition of the theme of the main plot. Instead it strengthens the main plot. The main features of the plot of *King Lear* is that it has two qualities—"re-inforcement" and "expansion". Both of these two functions are carried out by the sub-plot. Every incident in the sub-plot does not only parallel a like incident in the main plot, but re-inforces it and thus expands the scope of the play. So, whereas both Lear and Gloucester are the victims of filial ingratitude, Gloucester's blindness is the physical counterpart of the mental blindness, i.e., the madness, of Lear. Again, Edgar pretends to be mad, and this pretence of madness re-inforces the real madness of Lear. Edgar once held an honourable position in society and was once well-off in the world, but is reduced to beggary now and this fact re-inforces the pitiable state of Lear who was once a king and has now been reduced through the ingratitude of his daughters to a state of helpless destitution. The storm in nature reinforces the storm in Lear's mind. When we see him on the heath he is indirectly describing the fury of the storm by apostrophising it:

> Blow, wind, and crack your cheeks! rage! blow!
> You cataracts and hurricanoes, spout
> Till you have drench'd our steeples, drown'd the cocks![15]

Then, a few lines later, the storm in nature is linked with the storm in his own mind. As yet this mental upheaval has not produced the chaos of madness, but the very fact that Lear can address the elements as he does, attributing human passions to them, is an indication of the fact that that his own passions are being kept under control with great difficulty:

> I tax you not, you elements, with unkindness;
> I never gave you kingdom, call'd you children,
> You owe me no subscription. Then let fall
> Your horrible pleasure.[16]

Not only the events but the characters also re-inforce the main action. All the characters, even the minor ones, continually comment on the main action and this feature gives great expansion to the main plot. What happens to Lear is something intensely personal but the comments of the other characters show how the personal events affect so many other characters as well. The background of a whole society, an entire country is being continually asserted. As a matter of fact much more than a country is involved, for Lear comes to symbolise Man against Universe, as has been already discussed (*Vide* Chapter 6, Theme and Chapter 7, the discussion on Lear, *supra*).

The character who contributes the most towards re-inforcing and the expansion of the main plot is Edmund. This had been pointed out by Dr. Johnson. That astute critic had realised that the sub-plot, which had been thought to be one of the weaknesses of the play, actually was a strong support to the message that was being conveyed by the play. Edmund, according to him, "is made to co-operate with the chief design" and to highlight the moral of the play.

Edmund is the villain of the sub-plot at first. Then he starts to affect the main plot and at the end, by ordering the execution of Lear and Cordelia he concludes his villainy. It is true that he undergoes a change of heart but this change does not affect the course of action in any way. We see him getting success in whatever he undertakes. First of all he gets his father to believe his false allegations against Edgar, then he manipulates events in such a way that Edgar is forced to flee the country (though, of course, he does not actually do so). Edmund wins the favour of the Duke of Cornwall and is taken on by him as a trusted follower. Then, by betraying his father he himself becomes the Earl of Gloucester. Now fortune smiles even more brightly on him and both Goneril and Regan fall in love with him. He sees his way opening to the throne of England. Quite cold-bloodedly he debates within himself which of the two sisters is likely to be the most effective stepping-stones for him:

Which of them shall I take?

> Both? one? or neither? Neither can be enjoy'd
> If both remain alive.[17]

He decides to wait till the battle is over and then he will manage things in such a way that the Duke of Albany will be killed. He will then marry one of the sisters and soon enough the royal crown will be his. There is no doubt in his mind that his side will win the battle. He has never failed so far and the thought of failure does not cross his mind. We have seen evil conquering over good in the play—embodied in Goneril, Regan and Cornwall and reinforced by Edmund, who goes onwards, from triumph to triumph.

Then comes the inevitable reversal. Edmund becomes the direct cause of the murder of Regan by Goneril and her own ensuing suicide. These latter events are brought about by the sub-plot and finally the villain is punished. He is dishonoured, discredited and exposed by the brother he had wronged. Evil is defeated, though is seemed to triumph at first. Edmund's progress and final fall illustrates the message of the play.

The message conveyed by a play corresponds to one of the six elements of tragedy as given by Aristotle—the element of Thought. Explaining the nature of this element he says:

> Third in order is Thought—that is, the faculty of saying what is possible and pertinent in given circumstances.... Thought...is found where something is proved to be nor to be or a general maxim is enunciated.[18]

This is the equivalent of the theme of, or the moral conveyed by, any work. Tragedy deals with the problem of the existence of evil in man's heart and in the world. The tragic hero, specially the Elizabethan tragic hero, violates moral laws, brings ruin upon others and has to be finally punished. In this play the tragic hero is not an evil character. He is, indeed, "more sinn'd against than sinning." It is Edmund who is the transgressor, the criminal. He re-inforces the main plot so that, after his death, when moral order is restored, Albany and Edgar are there to pick up the pieces and begin a new life. Shakespeare, thus as Dr. Johnson says, uses two plots:

to impress this important moral that villainy is never at a stop, that crimes lead to crimes and at last terminate in ruin.[19]

There is also the view that *King Lear* has a unified plot and this unity of structure is the relationship of the two plots. King Lear makes an error of judgement right in the beginning of the play. He makes three errors: (i) error in understanding the nature of love, (ii) in understanding the nature of kingship, and (iii) in understanding the nature of language (*Vide* Chapter 7, the analysis of King Lear's character, *supra*). These errors, moreover, are such as do not affect merely his own mind or family, but an entire kingdom:

> ...they are the terrible mistakes of a man of action. Lear imposes on his world his erroneous conclusions about children and court.[20]

Conversely, in the sub-plot, Gloucester's troubles are imposed on him by Edmund. He starts to deceive his father without any provocation. It is not that his father had done anything to start him off in the reprehensible course of action he adopts. His villainy is the result of his ambition and frustrations, and there are no scruples in him:

> Gloucester is the object of manipulations; his error of understanding is that he too easily falls under the influence exercised upon him.[21]

Just as King Lear does not understand the deception practised upon him, so Gloucester fails to recognise his son till the very last moment. He thinks that he is worldly – wise and learned in the meanings of signs and portents, yet he passively accepts whatever is done to him. It is not surprising that he should look upon himself and other men as victims of the gods:

> As flies to wanton boys are we to th'gods
> They kill us for their sport.[22]

Thus, in every way, Gloucester's troubles show but another facet of the same miseries that have befallen Lear. The main plot and the sub-plot, in other words, are two sides of the same coin and this is the secret to the unity of the play:

Thus Lear and Gloucester are, in terms of structure, not duplicates, but complements: this is one key to the unity of *King Lear*.[23]

Analysing the plot of *King Lear*, John Holloway gives a different interpretation. To him the action of the play is not *action*, but *protraction*:

> ...taking note of something both plain and remarkable about the action of the play: what might be called not its *action* but its *protraction*.[24]

He finds that in this play there is no end to suffering and that the suffering is more prolonged than in the other tragedies. One tragic movement, as he says, more or less ends in Act IV, for her we have already had *peripeteia*, as Lear has fallen from the state of a king to that of the helpless victim of treachery and cruelty. His eyes have already been opened to his own folly. This is not all. He has learnt to recognise his own indifference to his subjects and he is full of remorse. He prays for them. In other words he is no longer pitying himself; instead he is pitying others:

> Poor naked wretches, wheresoe'er you are,
> That bide the pelting of this pitiless storm,
> How shall your houseless heads and unfed sides,
> Your loop'd and window'd raggedness defend you
> From seasons such as these?[25]

It would seem that by the end of the fourth Act the play has reached its destined end. But this is not the case, for suffering is prolonged even further both in the main and in the sub-plot. Lear recovers his reason only to be imprisoned. Every time whatever happens is worse than what has already happened. It is a saga of unending suffering.

This prolongation of suffering leads one to think that there is no end to suffering in this world – it ends only with death. This feeling is accentuated at the end of the play. The other tragedies sound the note of regeneration at the end. They propagate the idea that evil will not triumph, that the vicious have been punished and moral order has been restored. This is not, according to this critic, the feeling produced by the ending of *King Lear*. This is made clear in the epilogue:

> The oldest hath borne most: we that are young
> Shall never see so much nor live so long.[26]

The structure of the whole play is thus an intensification of suffering, with the under-running idea that one has to face it as best one may:

> Men must endure
> Their going hence, even as their coming hither:
> Ripeness is all.[27]

All these features lead to the conclusion that Shakespeare is trying to complete a design, a certain pattern in his tragedies. We are being repeatedly shown a man going through a certain set pattern of events and nowhere is this more clear than in *King Lear*. In the beginning the protagonist is at the top of the ladder, a king of kings. Then there come the trials of protracted suffering and we are led to ultimately discern:

> Something which might be called the vertebrate structure of its intrinsic design; the developing line, unabridged, of a human sacrifice.[28]

Another point of view interprets the plot of *King Lear* in terms of rhetoric, particularly the feature of its possessing two plots:

> Indeed, it may be possible to regard the double plot as a developing metaphor, opening up the principal action into two parts that mirror each other.[29]

A metaphor is a figure of speech in which a certain similarity is seen between two dissimilar objects. Likewise *King Lear* presents two plots in which two different characters undergo, almost simultaneously, two different sequences of events. The characters are different—one is a king, the other is a subject; in one case there are daughters, in the other there are sons. The events are different—in one case we have the renouncing of a kingdom and the loss of everything, including sanity, whereas in the other we have the forcible wresting of one's duchy and the loss of eyesight. Yet these differences are but superficial ones and the two plots are reflections of each other. Both of the protagonists undergo betrayal and suffering, are re-united to their children and die at the end. The surface dissimilarity does but underline the intrinsic similarity of the two plots. The two together make up one whole unified metaphor that highlights an entire philosophy of life and gives the play its structure.

There are, thus, many points of view from which the plot of *King Lear* has been studied. Only a few of them have been discussed above. Though dramatic structure is a rather technical aspect of plays, even this has produced a great variety of interpretations.

The Madness of Lear

Lear's madness occupies a very important position in the play. Madness, real or feigned, was one of the usual features of Elizabethan tragedies. There is madness in Kyd's *The Spanish Tragedy*, derived from Seneca, and since Kyd's tragedy became a generally accepted prototype, later plays also have the element of madness in them. Sometimes, it is pretended, as in Hamlet and in Edgar, but sometimes it is real as in Lear and many other characters, whether in Shakespeare or other writers. Madness served many dramatic purposes in these plays. Pretended madness often helped a character to veil his real motives, as is the case with Kyd's hero Hieronymo. In *King Lear* Edgar's pretended madness helps to disguise him and thus enables him to avoid getting arrested. Real madness always signifies the final breakdown of order into chaos. Sometimes, real madness is the result of great grief and sometimes, as in *King Lear* the causes are far more complex. Lear's madness, indeed, shows how subtle drama had become in about a decade:

> What separates Hieronymo from Lear is the fact that the latter's madness passes from the emotional to the intellectual and, indeed, the metaphysical plane.[30]

This metaphysical implication of Lear's madness is not a far-fetched interpretation, for modern readers all agree on this evaluation. So far as stagecraft goes, it should be remembered that the Elizabethan audience expected madness to be

entertaining. It is only in the modern age, particularly from the
late nineteenth century onwards that Lear's madness has been
treated very seriously by literary critics. According to some,
madness actually makes Lear more perceptive. He can now see
the truth to which his egotism had formerly made him so
blind:

> Through tatter'd clothes small vices do appear;
> Robes and furr'd gowns hide all. Plates in with gold,
> And the strong lance of justice hurtles breaks;
> Arm it in rags, a pigmy's straw does pierce it.
> None does offend, none—I say, none.[31]

The strong assertion in the last line shows an all-inclusive
tolerance which the sane and powerful king of the first scene
had not been capable of. He had been impatient of the good
advice offered by Kent and had banished him.

Moreover, there is no capacity for concealment in a
madman, so we see his mental processes quite clearly. Lamb,
referring to Lear's mad speeches, had pointed out this
psychological significance. Lear's madness, according to Lamb,
has lifted him up above the plane of ordinary sufferings that
can be inflicted on a man by either hostile nature or by other
humans:

> It is his mind which is laid bare...for we are Lear, we are in
> his mind, we are sustained by a grandeur which baffles the
> malice of daughters and storms.[32]

It is paradoxical that it is when his mind has become deranged
that Lear becomes the most perceptive. Madness brings real
comprehension to him, just as blindness brings true insight to
Gloucester. This fact had been realised quite early by serious
readers, and, indeed, Shakespeare himself hints at it through
the speeches, comments and asides of those other characters
who are present on the stage with Lear during these mad-
scenes. Clemen has summed up:

> Lear's insanity should not be dismissed as simple craziness.
> It is rather another manner of perception.[33]

When the seriousness of the implications of this madness is
taken for granted many other points of view can be easily

understood. The most serious of the interpretations of this madness is a religious one and this is the one which is generally accepted now. According to this view his madness purges Lear of all the impurities in his character so that after his cure he is a new and reformed person. There has been a moral regeneration in him. All the dross has been burned away and what remains is pure gold:

> His madness marked the end of the wilful, egotistical monarch. He is resurrected as a fully human being.[34]

This complete purification enables Lear later to admit his folly and gives him true humility so that he can ask forgiveness of the child he had wronged. It also enables him to make little of imprisonment. He has passed through such experiences as would make a prison paradise for him:

> Come, let's away to prison;
> We two alone will sing like birds i'th'cage:
> When thou dost ask me blessings, I'll kneel down,
> And ask forgiveness.[35]

Apart from this highly serious interpretation of Lear's madness there are several others. It has been said, for example, that madness comes upon Lear as a punishment according to tradition. He is a man who is naturally impatient and choleric. Kent, in the first scene, had hardly launched on his protests before he becomes impatient and rebukes him. He knows he can be terrible in his anger and easily ruin others, and this is exactly what he does with Kent. This impatience and anger lead him to commit his several errors of judgement in that scene. After that, when subjected to insult as well as cruelty, he is furiously angry—angry with his ungrateful daughters. He does not easily see his own faults. It is because of this anger that madness comes upon him. The angry and impatient old man is a traditional figure in Elizabethan drama and Elizabethan theories of psychology. Lear is an extreme case and therefore an extreme punishment is meted out to him:

> According to the traditional irascible-concupiscible distinction, Lear's intellectual error of anger receives the conventional punishment of madness.[36]

REFERENCES

1. Butcher, S.H., *op. cit.*, p. 23.
2. Holloway, J., *op. cit.*, p. 215.
3. Act III, sc.iv, ll. 32-33, p. 108.
4. Act IV, sc.vii, ll. 60-64, p. 179.
5. Bradbrook, M.C., *Themes and Conventions of Elizabethan Tragedy.* Cambridge: C.U.P., 1969 rpt., p. 67.
6. Muir, K., *op. cit.*, p. 219. The spelling has been modernised by the present writer for the convenience of the modern student.
7. *Ibid.*, p. 224. The spelling has been modernised.
8. *Ibid.*, p. 230. Spelling modernised.
9. Bradley, *op. cit.*, p. 203.
10. *Ibid.*
11. *Ibid.*, p. 205.
12. *Ibid.*, p. 207.
13. *Ibid.*, p. 211.
14. Spencer, T., *Shakespeare and the Nature of Man.* Cambridge: The University Press, 1945, p. 142.
15. Act III, sc.ii, ll. 1-3, pp. 99-100.
16. Act III, sc.ii, ll. 16-19, p. 101.
17. Act V, sc.i, ll. 57-59, pp. 184-85.
18. Butcher, S.H., *op. cit.*, p. 29.
19. Kermode, F., *op. cit.*, p. 28.
20. Heilman, Robert B., *The Unity of King Lear,* in Kermode, *op. cit.*, p. 171.
21. *Ibid.*
22. Act IV, sc.i, ll. 36-37, p. 140.
23. Heilman, *op. cit.*, p. 173.
24. Holloway, J., *King Lear* in Kermode, *op. cit.*, p. 215.
25. Act III, sc.iv, ll. 28-32, p. 108.
26. Act V, sc.v, ll. 324-25, p. 206.
27. Act V, sc.ii, ll. 9-11, p. 186.
28. Holloway, J., *op. cit.*, p. 227.
29. Elton, W.R., *Double Plot in King Lear,* in Kermode F., *op. cit.*, p. 256.
30. Fluchère, F., *op. cit.*, p. 244.
31. Act IV, sc.vi, ll. 162-66, pp. 168-69.
32. Kermode, F., *op. cit.*, p. 44.
33. Clemen, W., *op. cit.*, p. 151.
34. Everett, Barbara, *The New King Lear,* in Kermode, *op. cit.*, p. 185.
35. Act V, sc.iii, ll. 8-11, p. 187.
36. Elton, W.R., *op. cit.*, p. 247.

10

Imagery in *King Lear*

The imagery of a play is an element that serves not only to beautify it but to render it more effective as well. This is an aspect of Shakespearean drama that has been studied in detail by modern scholars. The function of his imagery, the relationship between the imagery and the theme, the development of his imagery in his dramatic career—all have been carefully studied and analysed, and explained.

Defining imagery, Henri Fluchère says:

Imagery may shortly be defined as a concrete illustration drawn upon by the poet to clarify or embellish the object that he seeks to describe.[1]

This definition however, does not cover Shakespeare's imagery effectively, for his images do not merely clarify or embellish, they have other functions as well.

It is often impossible to differentiate between rhetorical figures, images and symbols. These are integrally related and overlap quite often. An image can be studied as a figure of speech and it might be elevated into a symbol as well. This characteristic has been mentioned by Fluchère:

No strict rule allows us to say at what point we pass from the plane of pure rhetoric, to the plane of pure psychology, and even the metaphysical plane, in the use of imagery.[2]

Moreover, depending on the method of categorisation, the same image will come under different categories, i.e., a sense-image will also be a nature image or a domestic image or any other. This is true of all images.

Among images, the most obvious and elementary are the sense-images. They correspond to the five human senses. Visual images refer to the eye, auditory images to the ear, olfactory images to the sense of smell, gustatory to taste and tactile to touch. Sense-images may exist independently, or may mix and mingle with each other, in which case the phenomenon will be known as synaesthesia.

Sense-images are the most obvious ones and *King Lear* is rich in them. As a matter of fact sense-images can hardly ever stand alone. They usually involve some other aspects of life. Thus here is one of the first images used by Lear:

> While we
> Unburthen'd crawl toward death.[3]

Here we have a visual image. As such it is a sense-image, but it is also the image of a child crawling, which is a nursery-image. This is the case with all sense-images, for they depend upon the fact that a certain object is being perceived through the senses, therefore, the image will also be related to that particular object. Lear's description of the portion of the kingdom allotted to Goneril contains visual as well as nature images:

> With shadowy forests and with champains rich'd
> With plenteous rivers and wide-skirted meads.[4]

All the images here are taken from bounteous nature and in addition they are visual images as well. Had the images been slightly more detailed, i.e., if the sound of waves made by the rivers been described, then auditory images would also have been involved.

An extraordinary visual image has been used by the Earl of Kent:

> See better, Lear; and let me still remain
> The true blank of thine eye.[5]

Here the eye itself is used together with a sporting image, for "blank" refers to the centre of the target used for archery. Thus again there are two images here.

Images taken from different walks of life are to be found throughout the play. We have astronomy in:

> By the sacred radiance of the sun
> ...   .
> By all the operation of the orbs
> From whom we do exist and cease to be.[6]

Here the King wants to emphasise his rejection of Cordelia and so he refers to the sun, the planets and the stars, thus giving the passage sublimity and a cosmic dimension. On the other hand, when a tender idea has to be expressed, humbler images are used equally effectively. Lear had thought of spending the rest of his life with Cordelia and so he uses the image of a nursery:

> I lov'd her most, thought to set my rest
> On her kind nursery.[7]

Imagery from archery is used to describe an action that is irrevocable. It is, however, not an uncommon image.

> The bow is bent and drawn; make from the shaft.[8]

This is only a small list of a few images taken from different walks of life, all from only one scene. The diligent student will find many other kinds of images in this and other scenes. They not only ornament diction but intensify it.

The prevalence of animal imagery in *King Lear* is one of its most effective features. An early scholar had, after a detailed study, found a hundred and thirty-three separate mentions of sixty-four different animals in the entire play. These animal images serve many different purposes. A philosophical dimension is given to the passage when the animal image shows man's position in the Great Chain of Being. Secondly, the animal images highlight the brutal nature of the evil characters, and, thirdly, they draw parallels between man's life and that of animals. Thus Lear says in sorrow:

> 'Twas this flesh begot
> Those pelican daughters.[9]

Here the imagery highlights the sub-human nature of Goneril and Regan, for pelican chicks, according to Elizabethan belief used to kill their parent. The most terrible animal image in the play is used by the Duke of Albany:

> Humanity must perforce prey on itself
> Like monsters of the deep.[10]

This unforgettable image serves all the three purposes that have been mentioned above. It gives a philosophical dimension to the passage in that men are seen to be like soulless monsters. They also highlight man's inherent brutality. Apart from this a clear parallel is drawn between men and animals by using a simile.

Caroline Spurgeon, in her study of Shakespearean imagery, points out that images concerned with the human body recur throughout the play. The most remarkable of these images is given by Lear when recovered from madness:

> Thou art a soul in bliss; but I am bound
> Upon a wheel of fire, that mine own tears
> Do scald like molten lead.[11]

These wonderful lines have fused together many different kinds of images. There is visual image of a man being tortured, tactile image ("scald like molten lead") machinery of the wheel and finally, religious overtones are brought in because the wheel is of fire, and this suggests the purification of a sinful soul in purgatory. All these are blended together to make a composite image.

The images concerning the human body are usually images of suffering and pain and this suffering and pain refer not just to Lear but to man himself. As has been repeatedly pointed out by literary critics, Lear is not just an individual figure but an eminently universal one and the images of torture serve to highlight this aspect, particularly when they are juxtaposed with the images of nature. Caroline Spurgeon points out:

> There is an overtone, running through the crisis of the tragedy, the fury of the elements, described, be it remarked, wholly in terms of the human being.[12]

Thus, in the storm-scene, Lear again and again addresses the elements and refers to them as human beings, e.g.:

> Blow winds, and crack your cheeks, rage, blow
> ...   .
> I never gave you kingdoms, called you daughters.[13]

Such personifying images always intensify dramatic effects. These apostrophes of Lear serve not only to acquaint us with the inclemency of the weather but also to underline the fact that he is maddened by anger and mortification (though, of course, not really and truly insane as yet).

W. Clemen is another critic who has studied the imagery of Shakespeare's plays in detail. His study has revealed the important fact that Shakespeare's use of imagery developed with his dramatic art. The images in the early plays serve to beautify the style but as his art matured, his imagery became more and more functional, more and more relevant to the theme, the action and the characters of the play:

> The more Shakespeare becomes a conscious dramatist, the more he employs them for dramatic purposes. The images gradually lose their purely "poetic", often extraneous nature, and become one of the dramatic elements.[14]

He analyses *King Lear* in detail and finds that in this play the imagery is highly functional:

> In *King Lear* action and image appear to be particularly clearly dependent upon each other and are reciprocally illuminating.[15]

Not only is the imagery highly functional in this play but, according to him, here the imagery has reached a completely new stage of development in that it has taken on some of the functions that belong to other aspects of the play. One of these functions, for example, is to relate the play to elemental superhuman forces. The curse on Goneril is one of the best examples of this function:

> You nimble lightnings, dart your blinding flames
> Into her scornful eyes! Infect her beauty,
> You fen-suck'd fogs, drawn up by the pow'rful sun,
> To fall and blister her![16]

There are many other important functions that the images carry out in *King Lear*. In the passage given above, for example, the images not only suggest the presence of superhuman forces but that they are responsive to human prayer. They also hint at the slow disintegration of Lear's reason.

Images, according to Clemen, also foreshadow events, pass moral comments on characters and their actions, comment on mankind in general and carry out a number of other functions. Judged from this point of view, many of the images of the first scene are prophetic, for they foreshadow future events. Thus when Lear says:

The bow is bent and drawn, make from the shaft.[17]

Clemen calls it "the first independent image of the scene" and points out how it proclaims the fact that Lear has already committed the irrevocable folly of resigning his powers, and will have to suffer the inevitable consequences of his action. A few lines later Kent clarifies the folly of his actions:

Kill thy physician, and the fee bestow
Upon thy foul disease.[18]

This image, like the former one, is a premonition of what Lear is going to suffer at the hands of his two elder daughters, and prepares the audience for the future.

The images employed by the Fool carry out an important function: that of making self-realisation possible for Lear. The King has been so full of self-importance that he has not had the awareness necessary to understand other people's views. The Fool can understand this and therefore talks to him in proverb and rhyming doggerel, with images that all the time hammer away at Lear's understanding. He uses simple homely images that serve the function of keeping him in touch with the simple realities of life:

It becomes the task of the Fool to express in epigrammatic images the unreality of Lear's behaviour, his self-deception and his error.[19]

A simple but effective example of this is seen as the Fool uses the image of the egg to symbolise the crown and how Lear has halved it:

Why, after I have cut the egg i'th' middle and eat up the meat, the two crowns of the egg. When thou clovest thy crown i'th' middle and goa'st it away both parts, thou bor'st thine ass on thy back o'er the dirt.[20]

In the next scene, trying to warn the King of the possibility of rejection at Regan's hands, the Fool employs the image of a snail:

Fool: I can tell why a snail has a house.

Lear: Why?

Fool: Why, to put's head in; not to give it away to his daughters, and leave his horns without a case.[21]

An extremely apt image, for a snail carries its own house on its back but Lear shall, in a little while, have no house of his own to shelter in. In addition to being a homely image that tries to bring his folly home to Lear, this is an animal image that draws a parallel between the condition of an animal and a human being.

The study of imagery, indeed, is a very interesting one and can never be really exhausted. Images can be purely ornamental or they can describe actions and thus be functional. They can, as in a mature play like *King Lear*, serve to reflect the mental condition of the speaker. At a higher level, they can relate man to universe or to God. All these different implications and many others, have been studied in detail, throwing light upon Shakespeare's creative processes.

REFERENCES

1. Fluchère, H., *op.cit.*, p. 167.
2. *Ibid.*, p. 167 as above.
3. Act I, sc.i, ll. 39-40, p. 5.
4. Act I, sc.i, ll. 63-64, p. 7.
5. Act I, sc.i, ll. 156-57, p. 13.
6. Act I, sc.i, ll. 109-10, p. 10.
7. Act I, sc.i, ll. 122-23, p. 11.
8. Act I, sc.i, line 143, p. 12.
9. Act III, sc.iv, ll. 73-74, p. 111.
10. Act IV, sc.ii, ll. 49-50, p. 146.
11. Act IV, sc.vii, ll. 45-47, p. 178.
12. Spurgeon, Caroline, *Shakespeare's Imagery*, New York, 1936, p. 342.
13. Act III, sc. ii, ll. 1 and 17, pp. 99, 101.

14. Clemen, W., *The Development of Shakespeare's Imagery*. London: Methuen, 77 rpt., p. 81.

15. *Ibid.*, p. 133.

16. Act II, sc.iv, ll. 162-65, pp. 87-88.

17. Act I, sc.i, line 143, p. 12.

18. Act I, sc.i, ll. 161-62, p. 14.

19. Clemen, *op. cit.*, p. 142.

20. Act I, sc.iv, ll. 155-91, p. 42.

21. Act I, sc.v, ll. 26-30, p. 54.

11

Poetic Style: Diction and Versification

Shakespeare's style reflects, not only his own poetic genius, but his age. In other words, it is a typical Elizabethan-Jacobean style. His style is an important aspect of his drama and has been studied in great detail. Thus the style reflects the man and the milieu and yet it is a style that suits each speaker, whatever kind of character he may be.

A typical feature of these plays is that they are a mixture of prose and verse. The noble characters who usually belong to the main plot, speak in verse and the humbler characters in prose. Thus there are many prose passages in our play, spoken by the Fool and by Edgar in his disguise of Poor Tom.

Poetic style has, in itself, two aspects: the diction and the versification. The two shall, by turn, be separately considered.

(a) Poetic Diction

Horace, in his *Ars Poetica*, had laid down the rules of poetic diction very clearly, and these were well-known in the Elizabethan times. According to Horace, not only should the diction vary with the genre of poetry, but from character to character. The diction of elegies should be different from the diction of love poems and both should differ from satire. In drama the diction of the speaker should suit the age, sex and social status of the speaker:

> It will make a great difference whether a god or a hero is speaking, a man of ripe years or a hot-headed youngster in the pride of youth, a woman of standing or an officious nurse, a rowing merchant or a prosperous farmer.[1]

This means that each man and woman has his or her own diction in accordance with his or her age, profession and cultural level. Horace has given different categories but these can be multiplied almost endlessly, with many sub-divisions. Whatever kind of character is speaking, the diction must suit him. Naturally, therefore, in later Elizabethan drama, diction became highly specialised. M.C. Bradbrook, commenting, says about this:

> The specific style for princes, for lovers, for clowns, was fixed.[2]

The poet, however, must keep certain things in mind, whatever kind of diction he might be using. The diction must be realistic, but in addition it must also be such as to persuade the readers or the audience and move him:

> The Elizabethan dramatist's style is one of impassioned poetic rhetoric, the two commonest functions of which are to persuade and to touch the emotions.[3]

Aristotle has also pointed out (*Vide* Chapter 9, Plot, the definition of tragedy, *supra*) that the poet must make use of rhetorical devices—it is an indispensable part of poetic diction. Ben Jonson, even though he uses the low style in *The Alchemist*, embellishes it with numerous figures of speech. He does the same when an aristocratic character, Sir Epicure Mammon, is speaking, in the elevated style. Rhetorical devices have to be employed, whether it is a servant who is speaking, or his master.

Figures of speech have been recommended by English writers who, naturally enough, followed in the footsteps of the classical critics. Thus George Puttenham declares:

> There is nothing so fitte for the poem as to be furnished with all the figures that be Rhetoricall and such as do most beautifie the language with eloquence.[4]

There are many other theories of diction. Horace, for example, recommends the use of newly-coined words as well as the revival of outmoded words. Shakespeare has made use of all the ideas known in his time.

(b) Diction in *King Lear*

Shakespeare's artistry continued to develop, in every way, over two decades. His art matured more and more as the years passed and in *King Lear* he was at the height of his powers. He adopted all the conventions current at the time and amply illustrated how they can be used to enhance his own effects. The use of prose as well as verse serves to distinguish between the noble character and the humble and this is to be found in all the plays of the time. It was also one of the rules that the diction be suited to the action taking place on the stage. This goes back to Aristotle:

> ...language enriched in a variety of ways and artistic devices appropriate to the several parts of the play.[5]

This implies that even the same character must not speak in the same manner in different situations. This rule is always observed by Shakespeare, though he does not observe the rule of the Unities. His characters not only speak in accordance with their personality but also in accordance with the demands of the prevailing situation. An excellent example of this is afforded by Edgar. He speaks differently with each disguise (*Vide* the discussion of Edgar's character in Chapter 7, *supra*). He speaks the blank verse used by the nobility in the beginning of the play. Then when he adopts the disguise of Poor Tom he speaks in disjointed prose. This versatility in changing the diction is the most remarkable in the mock suicide scene. Here, at first, he speaks in wonderful blank verse when describing the cliff of Dover and the sea to the blind Gloucester. Then when Oswald comes he speaks in peasant dialect and then afterwards he reverts back to his former elevated language. Lear, when cursing Goneril, uses elevated and extremely strong diction but in the re-union scene and later just before he goes to prison he uses a gentle and soft diction. Throughout the play, moreover, the language is embellished with different rhetorical devices, as is fully in keeping with Aristotle's and Horace's dicta. Some of these shall be studied now.

Stylistic Devices

A rich variety of stylistic devices is to be found in *King*

Lear. Imagery and figures of speech are but two of them. Of
these two, imagery has been briefly discussed in the foregoing
chapter and now a few of the most important rhetorical
figures will be taken up. Most of the examples will be taken,
as in the case of imagery, from the first scene of the play
except a few important ones occurring elsewhere.

Similes are the most obvious figures of speech and the
easiest for the student to spot. The first two similes used in the
play are very short ones and do not call attention in themselves.
Both are spoken by the two elder sisters. Thus Goneril says
that she loves Lear.

As much as child e'er loved or father found.[6]

Regan says:

I am made of that self-same metal as my sister.[7]

Much more effective similies are used later in the play. Kent,
for example, uses a simile that is more than it looks:

A very honest-hearted fellow, and as poor as the King.[8]

This is an apt simile, but it is also an oxymoron, as "poor"
and "King" are mutually contradictory terms.

Metaphors have always been Shakespeare's favourite figure
of speech and they are liberally scattered throughout the play.
One such highly effective metaphor is used with animal
imagery:

'twas this flesh begot
Those pelican daughters.[9]

This metaphor is a particularly apt one, for it implies, not
merely that the daughters, like the chicks of pelicans, wound
the bosom of the mother, but also that the mother pelican
sacrifices her life for the sake of her chicks. This was a well-
known belief of his time and this metaphor is an instance of
how the poet uses popular belief to enhance poetic effect.
Another memorable metaphor is also used by Lear in a line
that has become justly famous:

Come not between the dragon and his wrath.[10]

This line, indeed, does not contain merely a metaphor, for it is
a more complex line, from a rhetorical point of view, than

appears at first. The Dragon might be, in addition to a metaphor, an allusion to the dragon of Britain:

> Lear may refer to the dragon of Britain, which he had
> to wear emblazoned on his helmet.[11]

The dragon is also used as a symbol of ferocity, in which case we have the substitution of a symbol for the thing symbolised, and this is metonymy. Again, "his wrath" actually means the object of his wrath, i.e., Cordelia, in which case we have the substitution of the abstract for the concrete, which means a synecdoche. This one line shows how rewarding a close study of diction can be, if only from the point of view of rhetoric, for in this line several figures of speech have been used simultaneously.

Shakespeare frequently uses figures of speech which are less familiar than simile and metaphor. For example there is a fine use of metonymy in the line:

> The vines of France and the milk of Burgundy.[12]

Here "vines" stand for wine, i.e., the cause substituted for the effect, and "milk" stands for pasture, i.e., the effect is substituted for the cause. In other words there are two metonymy in one line.

Antithesis also abounds in the play. In the first scene itself the King of France uses several of them:

> Fairest Cordelia, that art most rich, being poor;
> Most choice, forsaken, and most lov'd, despis'd![13]

Here three antitheses occur in quick succession. The accumulation makes the speech all the more effective.

King Lear is one of those plays in which, more perhaps than in any other, apostrophes and invocations play a crucial part. The first of them occurs in Edmund's speech:

> Thou Nature, art my goddess; to thy law
> My services are bound.[14]

This is not a very remarkable apostrophe. They become the most intense in Lear's diatribes:

> Hear, Nature, hear! dear Goddess, hear!

> Suspend thy purpose, if thou didst intend
> To make this creature fruitful.[15]

This passage contains, in its entirety, five sentences, each of them an invocation to Nature, pleading with her to punish Goneril. This is the first of such passages. The careful student will find many more of them later and most of the apostrophes are addressed to nature.

Rhetorical questions give a dramatic quality to diction, specially when used in great number, as Edmund does in his first soliloquy:

> For that I am some twelve or fourteen moonshines
> Lag of a brother? Why bastard? Wherefore base?
> When my dimensions are as well compact,
> My mind as generous, and my shape as true,
> As honest madam's issue? Why brand they us
> With base? with baseness? bastardy? base, base?[16]

In the few lines quoted here there are eight rhetorical questions in just six lines. It is a very effective speech.

There are many such figures of speech strewn throughout the play and all serve to make the style complex and effective. In Shakespeare's mature work figures of speech are not employed as mere ornaments they are highly functional, serving to highlight the strong resentment, of violent protestations or aggressive mood of the speaker.

Apart from rhetoric many other stylistic devices are used by poets. One such device is the allusion. These are of many kinds—classical allusion, Biblical allusion, topical allusion, etc. All these, and more, can be found in *King Lear*, and in great number. The King of France's splendid antitheses, besides being rhetorically rich, contain a Biblical reference as well and this gives them depth of meaning:

> As poor, yet making many rich; as
> having nothing, yet possessing all things.[17]

The King of France repeats these antitheses almost word for word in his apostrophe to Crodelia:

> That art most rich, being poor;
> Most choice, forsaken; and most lov'd, despised.[18]

Alongside numerous Biblical allusions there are the equally numerous classical allusions. These are of mainly two kinds: allusions to classical authors, and to classical mythology. Cordelia's answers in the love-test and Lear's reaction is one of the most well-known classical allusions in Shakespeare:

Cordelia: Nothing, my lord.

Lear: Nothing?

Cordelia: Nothing

Lear: Nothing will come of nothing: speak again.[19]

This harks back to the old Latin proverb *"ex nihilo nihil fit"* (nothing comes of nothing) which had been repeated by many writers, classical as well as English.

Likewise, there are allusions to classical mythology specially in swearing:

Lear: Now, by Apollo—

Kent : Now by Apollo, King, Thou swear'st thy gods in vain.[20]

This invocation to Apollo is specially ironical, as Apollo is the god of wisdom and Lear is acting in a particularly unwise manner. Moreover, Lear's father Oladul according to Geoffrey of Monmouth fell on the temple of Apollo and broke his neck and was killed.

Shakespeare uses topical allusions very frequently to increase the popular appeal of his passages. These are more plentiful in comedy than in tragedy, but there is a specially fine one in *King Lear*. Lear, in his madness, takes Edgar for one of his hundred knights and takes exception to his dress. Edgar, disguised as Poor Tom, is wearing only a blanket:

...only I do not, like the fashion of your garments, you will say they are Persian, but let them be chang'd.[21]

This reference to Persian robes is more complex than it appears to be. First of all, a Persian, in Elizabethan times was taken to be a wise man, a magus, and mad Lear addresses Edgar as a wise man. Furthermore, a Persian embassy had come recently to the court of King James and the men of London had had the opportunity to become acquainted with the flowing robes of Persians. An allusion of this type a joke on the outlandish dress would naturally be popular.

Proverbs serve to lend point to the diction and there are many such to be found in *King Lear*. The majority of these is spoken by the Fool—they occur so often in his speech that it can be said to be his very way of speaking. Other characters also use them:

> Kent: Thou out of heaven's benediction com'st
> To the warm sun![22]

To come out into the sun is not a proverb which is much in use today, but it was well-known those days, applied to those who were turned out of house and home and had to depend entirely on the common benefits of the air and sun.

Besides these, there are allusions to commonly accepted folk tales and beliefs. These are to be found mostly in Edgar's speeches when, as Poor Tom, he continually refers to popular beliefs. Samuel Harsnett's work *A Declaration of Egregious Popish Impostures* was one of his sources, not for plot, but for these references. Edgar's demonology is derived from this work. He is continually referring to fiends. Sometimes, he is just describing them and at times they are calling to him:

1. This is the foul fiend Flibbertigibbet: he begins at curfew and walks till the first cock.[23]

2. The Prince of Darkness is a gentleman; Modo he is called, and Mahu.[24]

3. Frateretto calls me, and tells me Nero is an angler in the lake of Darkness.[25]

4. Hoppedance cries in Tom's belly for two white herrings.[26]

All these names of devils have been taken from Harsnett's book, which describes their characteristics as well:

> Captaine Maho, Saras devil, Captaine
> Modu, Maynies devil.
> Frateretto, Fliberdigibbet, Hoberdidance.
> The Prince of hel...Hoberdicut.[27]

Shakespeare changes the names slightly, nor does he describe them, but they serve to make Edgar's speeches wild enough to pass muster.

These discussions of a few of the most obvious stylistic devices used by Shakespeare to enhance his diction make one realise how rich his language is.

(c) Versification

As has been pointed out in the beginning of this chapter, diction and versification are but two different sides of the same coin—poetic style. They go hand in hand with each other and supplement each other. No account of Shakespeare's poetic style can be complete without a mention of this aspect of his work. This, however, is a rather technical subject and a rudimentary knowledge of prosody is essential to understand this aspect of his art.

As has been pointed out, both prose and verse were used in Elizabethan drama. Blank verse as well as couplets were used in poetry. Blank verse is a passage of unrhyming pentametre lines in iambic metre. This is a disyllabic metre, of which the first syllable is unstressed and the second is stressed:

Ă sér / vănt thát / hĕ bréd / thrĭlled wíth / rĕmórse,

Ŏppós'd / ăgaínst / thĕ aćt / beňdiňg/hĭs swórd

To hís / gřeat más / tĕr who / thĕreát / eňrag'd

Flew oň/him, aňd/ămoňgst / thĕm fell'd / hĭm deád.[28]

This passage has four unrhyming iambic pentametre lines and is thus an example of perfect blank verse. Passages of such metrical regularity are very difficult to find, for usually there are trochaic and anapaestic feet mixed with iambics and this mixture gives variety to the verse, saving it from a mechanical regularity that would soon become monotonous.

There are many variations to be noted in dramatic blank verse. The lines, for example, can be end-stopped lines or run-on ones. In the passage given above the lines are not end-stopped. The actor, while declaiming them, does not have to stop at the end of the line but goes on to recite the next. Sometimes, however end-stopped lines are deliberately used for greater effect. Lear is speaking to Goneril:

> I prithee, daughter, do not make me mad.
> I will not trouble thee, my child; farewell.
> We'll no more meet, no more see one another.
> But yet thou art my flesh, my blood, my daughter;
> Or rather, a disease that's in my boil.[29]

This terrible passage goes on for fourteen lines and each line is an end-stopped line. Lear, stopping at the end of each line, emphasises the idea expressed in it. Each line is like a hammer-blow. There are clear punctuation marks at the end of each line—comma, colon, etc., so the actor declaiming the lines will have to stop briefly at the end of each. Moreover, this feature of the passage makes it clear that Lear, though he is mortified and angry, is yet keeping his passions under control. It is with great difficulty that he is controlling himself and so he has to speak slowly and deliberately, stopping at the end of each line.

An important aspect of blank verse is the caesura or the medial pause. This is a brief pause made within the blank verse line to make the sense clear as well as to make it more flexible. If this pause or caesura occurs at the same place in every line then the passage becomes like a mechanical jingle, to be avoided in blank verse at all costs. The well-versed poet, therefore, alters the position of the caesura, as in the passage given below:

> Let it be so! ‖ thy truth then be thy dower!
> For ‖ by the sacred radiance of the sun,
> The mysteries of Hecate ‖ and night.[30]

The double vertical lines indicate the caesurae. Thus, in the first line of the passage quoted above the caesura falls after the fourth syllable, but in the second line it falls after the first. In the third line it falls after the seventh syllable. There is, thus, great variety in the placing of the caesurae which in its turn gives flexibility to the lines. Sometimes, there are two caesurae in a line. Thus Lear says:

> As here I give
> Her father's heart from her! ‖ Call France ‖ who stirs?[31]

Double caesurae are not very usual in blank verse. Here it serves to make the line dramatic, as there is a command in it, which requires a pause before and after.

Blank verse, by definition, contains five feet or ten syllables. The poet, however, has great liberty, and in order to make his poetry, more effective, can make the line short or long as he likes. Shakespeare makes most effective use of a truncated line:

> And, to deal plainly.
> I fear I am not in my perfect mind.[32]

Here the half-line demands a long pause before Lear, in a hesitant manner, can bring himself to admit that perhaps he is not fully sane even now. Shakespeare repeatedly achieves wonderful effects with his half lines:

> The gods are just, and of our pleasant vices
> Make instruments to plague us.[33]

This half-line, consisting of only three feet, requires a long pause, allowing the observation to sink in.

Stichomythia is a device that gives flexibility or precision to a dialogue. Sometimes different characters each speak one line and sometimes different characters cut in upon each other and speak in the same line, breaking it up into two or more parts. Both can be found in the passage given below:

Lear: But goes thy heart with this?

Cordelia: Ay, my good lord.

Lear: So young, and so untender?

Cord.:   So young, my lord, and true.[34]

Here the first line is broken up into two parts as both Lear and Cordelia speak in it. The next two lines consist of quick question and answer. Both are half lines, for the first one has seven syllables and the second only six, yet they are counted as full lines. Shakespeare's great mastery over the medium of dramatic blank verse can easily be surmised when such deliberate irregularities are made to serve the purpose of heightening the dramatic effect.

Apart from blank verse, there is frequent use of couplets. The tradition of using couplets is derived from Seneca, who used them particularly to stress moral concepts. Shakespeare uses couplets very frequently, sometimes in order to sum up the theme, sometimes underlining important sentiments, sometimes for other specific purposes. Thus Kent, after being banished delivers an eight-line passage in couplets:

> Fare thee well, King, sith thus thou wilt appear,
> Freedom lives hence, and banishment is here.[35]

Of these four couplets spoken by Kent, the first one as quoted above is addressed to Lear, the second to Cordelia, the third to Goneril and Regan and the fourth to the courtiers. Each couplet is like a hammer-blow, commenting upon the action of the King and his daughters.

The most important passage in Couplets is the Fool's prophecy:

> When priests are more in word than matter;
> When brewers mar their malt with water;
> When nobles are their tailors' tutors;
> No heretics burn'd but wenches' suitors;[36]

This passage contains a total of seven couplets. Each line is end-stopped. It is purported to be a prophecy to be uttered by Merlin. The Fool pretends to be a prophet who existed before Merlin. These lines are thought to be a parody of some lines supposed to have been written by Chaucer.[37]

Music, both instrumental and vocal, plays a significant part in Shakespeare's plays. There are quite a few songs in *King Lear*, sung by the Fool and by Edgar in his persona of Poor Tom. W. Clemen is of the opinion that both the imagery and the songs of the Fool create a sense of detachment:

> The little songs which the Fool sings further enhances this quieting effect which liberates us and creates this detachment.[38]

Everyone, however, may not agree with this.

The Fool sings ten songs. They are not such songs as can be called well-constructed lyrics. They are more like doggerels, without the beauty of expression and imagery which is a hallmark of Shakespearean lyrics. What they lose in beauty, however, they gain in meaning, for almost all of them refer, obliquely or directly, to Lear's folly and his present situation. The first such song is but a string of proverbs and metrically very irregular. In the beginning there are three couplets in a metre not usually found in English poetry—amphibrach:

Hăve móre thăn / thou shówest,

Spĕak leśs thăn / thŏu knówest,

Lĕnd leśs thăn / thŏu owest,

Rĭde móre thăn / thŏu góest.[39]

It does not, however, keep up this uniformity in metre or in length, for the last three lines of the song are most irregular. As a matter of fact, none of the songs in the play, be it sung by the Fool or by Edgar, is at all like a typical Shakespearean song. When they are contrasted with songs like "come away, come away death" (*Twelfth Night*), "When daisies pied" (*The Winter's Tale*) or "Full fathom five" (*The Tempest*) the difference becomes amply clear. Compared with such lyrics the songs in *King Lear* seem to be mere doggerels. Their actual value lies, not in lyrical beauty, but in the meaning they try to communicate to Lear.

REFERENCES

1. Dorsch, T.S., ed. and transl., *Classical Literary Criticism*, Penguin Books, 1975, p. 83.

2. Bradbrook, M.C., *The Growth and Structure of Elizabethan Comedy*. Cambridge: C.U.P., 1954, p. 45.

3. Fluchère, H., *op. cit.*, p. 152.

4. Quoted by Fluchère, *op. cit.*, p. 159.

5. Dorsch, T.S., *op. cit.*, p. 39.

6. Act I, sc.i, line 58, p. 6.

7. Act I, sc.i, line 68, p. 7.

8. Act I, sc.iv, ll. 19-20, p. 35.

9. Act III, sc.iv, ll. 73-74, p. 111.

10. Act I, sc.i, line 121, p. 11.

11. Muir, K., *op. cit.*, p. 11.

12. Act I, sc.i, line 83, p. 8.

13. Act I, sc.i, ll. 249-50, p. 19.

14. Act I, sc.ii, ll. 1-2, p. 22.

15. Act I, sc.iv, ll. 273-75, p. 48.

16. Act I, sc.ii, ll. 5-10, p. 23.

17. St. Paul's second Epistle to the Corinthians, Chapter 6, v.10. *The Holy Bible.* New York: American Bible Society, p. 186.

18. Act I, sc.i, ll. 249-50, p. 19.

19. Act I, sc.i, ll. 86-89, p. 9.

20. Act I, sc.i, ll. 158-60, p. 13.

21. Act III, sc.vi, ll.77-79, p. 127.

22. Act III, sc.ii, ll. 157-58, p. 74.

23. Act III, sc.iv, ll. 112-13, p. 115.

24. Act III, sc.iv, ll. 140-41, p. 117.

25. Act III, sc.vi, ll. 6-7, p. 122.

26. Act III, sc.vi, ll. 30-31, p. 124.

27. Muir, K., *op. cit.*, p. 240.

28. Act IV, sc.ii, ll. 73-76, p. 149.

29. Act II, sc.iv, ll. 216-221, p. 91.

30. Act I, sc.i, ll. 107-09, p. 10.

31. Act I, sc.i, line 125, p. 11.

32. Act IV, sc.vii, ll. 62-63, p. 179.

33. Act V, sc.iii, ll. 169-70, p. 197.

34. Act I, sc.i, ll. 104-06, p. 10.

35. Act I, sc.i, ll. 179-80, p. 15.

36. Act III, sc.i, ll. 81-84, p. 105.

37. Muir, K., *op. cit.*, p. 104n.

38. Clemen, W., *op. cit.*, p. 144.

39. Act I, sc.iv, ll. 116-19, p. 40.

Critical Reception of *King Lear*

King Lear has, from the very beginning, been an extremely challenging play for the stage. It always has a very strong impact on the audience when performed on the stage, but an even stronger one on the sensitive reader. This had led to the supposition, expressed the best by Lamb, that it is too great to be acted on the stage:

> Lear is essentially impossible to be represented on the stage.[1]

This is because, on reading, the play impresses the reader as dealing with something that goes far beyond ordinary life, far beyond what can be presented on the stage. The highly sophisticated actors and directors of the twentieth century are specially conscious of this:

> A mountain whose summit has never been reached....
> Olivier here, Laughton there: it's frightening.[2]

King Lear is the least actable of the four plays. As far as its stage-history is concerned, the most important chapter concerns the adaptation made by Nahum Tate in 1681. He rewrote it and made several changes in the play that are quite unacceptable to the modern audience. There is, for example, a love-affair between Cordelia and Edgar. The King of France has been omitted and, what is far more serious, the Fool has been omitted. What most outrages the sophisticated modern audience as well as the reader, is that a happy ending is supplied. This alters the very genre of the play. Instead of being one of the greatest, perhaps the greatest tragedy of the poet, it becomes a comedy. These are the most significant changes but there are several other minor ones. These changes reflect not just Tate's whims, but the contemporary attitude to the play. The late seventeenth century audience thirsted after the elements of romance and poetic justice, both of which are totally absent from the play, and Tate's version gave these in ample measure. This version became highly popular. So much so that it held the stage for a century and a half, with great writers like Garrick, Kemble, Kean and others acting in six great appearances. The original text was almost completely restored, but this was done more than a century later, in 1838, by which time the Romantic Movement had brought about a thorough change.

In the eighteenth century serious literary reading and criticism of Shakespeare was undertaken by many critics, the foremost of them being Dr. Johnson. Tate had supplied the play with a happy ending at the end of the seventeenth century. This has been, along with many other features of his version, ridiculed as well as stringently criticised, but it should not be forgotten that one of the very first serious critics of Shakespeare had objected to the ending. Dr. Johnson could not defend this aspect of the play:

> Since all reasonable beings naturally love justice, I cannot easily be persuaded that the observation of justice makes a play worse.[3]

This attitude was inevitable in an age which valued the moral element as much as the classical elements in a play. A century later, in an age which put equal value on psychological insight and imaginative interpretation, we see a sensitive critic shifting the focus of criticism. New horizons are being discovered, new outlooks are being adopted now by the Romantic critics. Thus, Lamb finds Tate's version to be preposterous:

> A happy ending! as if the living martyrdom that Lear had gone through, the flaying of his feelings alive, did not make a fair dismissal from the stage the only decorous thing for him.[4]

By this time, the imaginative power of the poet and the

impact on the reader's imagination is being taken into serious consideration and criticism has become highly personal. Coleridge's analysis of the play is by far the most systematic and objective criticism of the Romantic period. Not only does he give his general impression of the play, but also detailed notes on the individual scenes. He points out how the main theme of the play is the inner world of Lear's stormy passions:

> After-insight into the mind and mood of the person whose character, passions and sufferings are the main *subject-matter* of the play.[5]

This shifting of the focus to the chaotic mental world is typical of Romantic criticism. Referring to the sufferings portrayed in the play, he voices some of the most irrefutable arguments ever advanced:

> If we want to witness mere pain, we can visit the hospital.... It is the representation of it, not the reality, that we require, and not the thing itself, and we pronounce it good or bad in proportion as the representation is an incorrect or a correct imitation. The true pleasure we derive from theatrical performances arises from the fact that they are unreal and fictitious.[6]

These remarks are highly illuminating and complex, for they combine Aristotle's demands with Romantic ideas.

In the twentieth century literary criticism branched out into many directions. First of all, the different elements of drama, like the plot, the characters etc. came to be studied separately and then, from the middle of the century onwards, different schools of literary criticism came into existence, each with its own theory and technique. A.C. Bradley's essay in the beginning of the century is a landmark in Shakespeare criticism. He analyses the plot, the characters, the theme, the element of madness etc. Most important of all, he listed the "improbabilities" in the play. This is an essay that no later critic can afford to ignore, for, within a small compass, Bradley manages to cover all the important aspects of the play. A very important aspect of his criticism is the religious interpretation he puts upon the play:

Should we not be at least as near the truth if we called this play *The Redemption of King Lear* and declare that the business of "the gods" with him is neither to torment him, nor to teach him "a noble anger" but to lead him to attain through apparently hopeless failure the very aim and end of life.[7]

This encouraged a religious interpretation of the play by later critics. Historians of criticism have labelled Bradley's criticism as "Romantic Expansionist Interpretation".

Interpretive criticism produced many important works, one of which is G. Wilson Knight's *King Lear and the Comedy of the Grotesque* in which he highlights the comic element in the play. Individual characters, particularly those of Lear and the Fool were studied in great detail (Enid Welsford, *The Fool in King Lear*). Critics became conscious of the relevance of Elizabethan philosophical background and interpreted the play by relating it to contemporary philosophical and psychological theories. Theodore Spencer in his *Shakespeare and the Nature of Man* gives this kind of analysis and so does W.R. Elton in an essay written much later, *The Double Plot in King Lear*. Aspects like imagery were taken up and studied in detail by Caroline Spurgeon and W. Clemen.

From the middle of the century onwards many different schools of criticism came into existence, and the plays of Shakespeare were taken up and studied in the light of these theories. The Absurdist attitude is concerned more with an attitude to life than a technique, and an Absurdist study of the play is given by Jan Kott. All these different theories serve to highlight the complexity and inexhaustibility of Shakespeare.

REFERENCES

1. Kermode, F., *op. cit.*, p. 45.
2. *Ibid.*
3. *Ibid.*, p. 29.
4. *Ibid.*, p. 45.
5. *Ibid.*, p. 34.
6. *Ibid.*, p. 42.
7. Bradley, A.C., *op. cit.*, p. 235.

Important Questions

1. Does the double-plot in *King Lear* truly constitute its weakness? Give reasons for your answer.

2. Can *King Lear* be called a comedy of the grotesque? Support your answer with reference to the text.

3. "*King Lear* is, like the *Paradiso*, a vast poem on the victory of true love." Elucidate.

4. Justify the term "Christian allegory" as applied to *King Lear*.

5. Can it be said that Lear is "a man more sinn'd against than sinning"? Support your answer with reference to the text.

6. "*King Lear* is at least as Christian as the *Divine Comedy*." Elucidate.

7. Scrutinise critically the statement that *King Lear* should be retitled "The Redemption of King Lear".

8. "Cordelia is Shakespeare's version of singleness and integrity." Elucidate.

9. Analyse Lear's character as that of the ideal tragic hero.

10. "The Fool is as wonderful a creature as Caliban—an inspired idiot." Comment with special reference to the text.

11. "Lear's intellectual error of anger receives the conventional punishment of madness." Elucidate.

12. Write a note on the imagery of *King Lear* with the necessary illustrations.

13. Write a note on the sub-plot of *King Lear*.

14. Write a note on Shakespeare's characterisation in *King Lear*.

15. Comment on Shakespeare's versification in *King Lear*.

Select Bibliography

Bayley, John, *Shakespeare and Tragedy*, Routledge & Kegan Paul, London, 1981.

Bradbrook, M.C., *Themes and Conventions of Elizabethan Tragedy*, Cambridge U.P., 1935.

—— *Elizabethan Stage Conditions*, Cambridge U.P., 1968.

Bradley, A.C., *Shakespearean Tragedy*, Macmillan, London, 1960.

Bratchell, D.F. (ed.), *Shakespearean Tragedy*, London, Routledge, 1990.

Campbell, Lily B., *Shakespeare's Tragic Heroes*, Cambridge U.P., 1930.

Clemen, W., *The Development of Shakespeare's Imagery*, London, Methuen, 1951.

Evans, B., *Shakespeare's Tragic Practice*, Oxford, U.P., 1978.

Florence, Horace Howard ed., *A New Variorum Edition of Shakespeare: King Lear*, New York, Dover Publications Inc., 1963.

Kermode, F. (ed.), *King Lear: A Casebook*, London, Macmillan, 1969.

Knight, G. Wilson, *The Wheel of Fire*, Oxford, Oxford U.P., 1938.

Lawlor, John, *The Tragic Sense in Shakespeare*, London, Chatto & Windus, 1960.

Leech, Clifford, *Shakespeare's Tragedies*, London, Chatto & Windus, 1950.

Muir, K. (ed.), *King Lear*, Arden Shakespeare, London, Methuen, 1972.

Ribner, I., *Patterns in Shakespearean Tragedy*, London, Meth., 1960.

Spencer, T., *Shakespeare and the Nature of Man*, New York, Macmillan, 1945.

Spurgeon, C., *Shakespeare's Imagery and What it Tells Us*, Cambridge University Press, 1935.

Wilson, Harold S., *On the Design of Shakespearean Tragedy*, Toronto University Press, 1957.

Index